BE AN
ICON

DISCOVER HOW ORDINARY PEOPLE
BECAME EXTRAORDINARY

KENNETH
NKEMNACHO

© 2014 Kenneth Nkemnacho
info@kennethvisionmedia.com
Published by Kenneth Vision Media
First Edition

ISBN: 978-0-9568373-7-0

All dictionary meanings were taken from
http://dictionary.reference.com

The stories in this book were adapted from:
www.psychologytoday.com
www.cnn.com
www.biography.com
www.aljazeera.com
www.nbcnews.com
www.nydailynews.com
www.ipsnews.net
www.forbes.com
How to live your dreams

DEDICATION

This book is dedicated to:
My wife - Ruth Abosede, My daughter - Favour Chibuzor,
My son - Joshua Nkemdiche.
Thank you for
walking the hard road with me

TABLE OF CONTENTS

INTRODUCTION

After writing any book, it is my usual practice that my wife must read it first, and offer her suggestions before I make a decision whether to publish or not. I honestly respect her opinions because they are valuable to me.

When I finished writing BE AN ICON, I asked her to read it. She was so excited as she read the first chapter, but while reading the second, I noticed that she was frowning. When I asked why, she said, 'I don't like the second chapter because it is too abstract.' The moment she said that, I knew that I had to restart the whole book because the structure and nature of the second chapter was that of the rest of the book.

For a few months, I began to think on how to redo the book, until one day, the idea hit me. So, what you're about to read is as a result of the thinking of a woman with a wise heart and mind.

BE AN ICON is a motivational, leadership, strategy, and personal development book. It contains diverse topics, but all directed towards a common result; success. The book is packed with principles that are applicable to every facet of life. It isn't a book for one-time read; it is a book that can be daily looked into, so as to daily, succeed.

BE AN ICON wasn't written to just give you a momentary motivation; it teaches you how to. If you know how to, you will understand the various steps to take in order to excel in your pursuits. The how to, is the difference between the first draft of this book and the final one. The first mainly motivated but didn't tell you what to do, but the second proffered solutions.

As you take the time to read this book, pay close attention to the principles, strategies, suggestions, and opinions; as this, will guide you and direct you to more purposeful paths that will bring that change and difference you've desired.

BE AN ICON will either change your thinking or boost it if you're already in the right direction. It will serve as a catalyst that will help speed up your reaction for positive change.

As you read, get a copy for someone. As you read, read with an open mind because an open mind is a creative mind.

Thank you.

Kenneth Nkemnacho

CHAPTER ONE

WHO IS AN ICON?

I was raised in a humble background; clouded by the chains of poverty and lack. Everything around me told me that there was no future because it all appeared like we were doomed to always be at the bottom of life. But, in the house was a believer; a woman who, in spite of lack of education and exposure saw the tomorrow that she knew was impossible for her to enter, but encouraged everyone who had age on his or her side to do so. This woman was my maternal grandmother; a unique icon emeritus!

In a stage that we couldn't afford a plate of boiled rice, my maternal grandmother, in her imagination, made you add salad and grilled chicken to the meal that was completely out of reach. As a growing child, the only future I saw was the picture painted and interpreted by my maternal grandmother; Alice. So, my impression of who an icon should be is:

A Mentor: a mentor is a careful guide and a teacher that sees a better tomorrow despite the upheavals of today. A mentor is someone who believes in the possibilities of the mentee breaking through the obstacles and chains of yesterday and today, and so, encourages the mentee to push on, until the baby of the dream and vision is born.

Everyone who succeeded, one way or the other, had someone who stood formally or informally, as a mentor. Every mentor who has a genuine interest in the success of the mentee is an icon. An icon does not have to be popular; he may just be someone in a hinterland, unknown to the world, but preparing the destiny and purpose of those that will be world changers. Are you an icon?

A Picture: a picture may be a painting or photograph. Whenever we encounter challenges, pictures always pop up in our minds. The picture you see may be the solution you need to overcome the obstacles you meet. Sometimes, the picture that appears in your mind when certain obduracy confronts you is that of an icon. The icon may be a book that you've read that deals with such challenge or a quote from someone you have met one way or the other. The crux of the matter is that a picture is an icon. So, when you face a circumstance or when a circumstance faces you, which picture do you see? The picture you see will either save or enslave you. On the other hand, when people encounter dangers in life, business or career, what kind of picture do they perceive you to be; a saviour or enslaver? A picture is an icon. Are you an icon?

An Image: an image is similar to a picture; the only difference is that some images are statues; therefore, they are in solid forms. Some people can't paint pictures, but they can mould statues. Well, I would rather say that unprofessionally speaking, everyone can at least paint or mould something even if it may look ugly and a complete contrast to what it should actually be. For the fact everyone can paint or mould; though it may appear shapeless, means that everyone has the capability of being an icon. An icon is an image; an image is a brand. As an icon, you are a brand. You are a far bigger brand than Coca-Cola. You are a much bigger brand than Apple. You are a far greater brand than all the products and services on earth combined. You are an image; a top class image. Treat yourself like a top brand because that is who you are!

A Representation: a representation is an expression or designation that stands on others behalf. A representation is also a description or statement of things that are true or alleged. An icon is a representation. As an icon, you stand for excellence and success. As an icon, you stand for courage and victory. When you see who you are, you will live who you are. As a representation, you may sometimes take the knock, but that is part of your assignment. Before writing this chapter, I copy edited a client's PH.D thesis on industrial relations. On it, I read a lot about union and non-unionised forms of employee representations. Those who represent employees in management/employee negotiations sometimes get battered by management for being reprobate. The reps don't surrender because of fear of intimidation or victimisation; they know that it is part of their jobs. Therefore, as someone who represents dreams and visions, don't hang up because of the battering. Remember, it is part of the assignment. You're an icon; you're a representation of excellence. Maintain your position; maintain your status.

A Symbol: some companies don't talk too much; their symbols speak for them. When I see the Nike symbol, I simply recite their slogan; Just do it! Whenever I see a network of rings of different colours; I remember the Olympics. Anytime I see the symbol of a grey apple with a small part of its side bitten off, I know it is the mega company, Apple; the owner of all the I's; iPod, iPhone, iPad, and whatever.

A symbol is the voice of a brand. You are a symbol, don't lose your voice. A symbol is the picture, image and representation of a brand. You are a picture, image and representation of a massive brand; be visible; be notable. As a symbol, you are an identity; don't hide it. As a symbol, you are a mind changing slogan; shout the slogan; make it loud. You've always been an icon even if you thought you weren't. Continue to be; you are an icon!

A Sign: a sign is a footprint that shows that you were there. When you leave this world, you may go with your symbol, but your sign will always remain if you actually made a difference. Symbols may go, but signs persist. Mohammed Ali does not have a symbol, but we see his signs everywhere. Nelson Mandela does not have a symbol, but his signs will live forever. Martin Luther King Junior does not have a symbol, but his signs still form the basis for human freedom. Are you a sign, or are you just a symbol? A true icon must have a sign. What is your sign?

A Figure: a figure, apart from its description as shape is a number. As an icon, you are a number. As an icon, you're not just an ordinary number; you are number one. As number one, you are the principal and head. A principal and head is an outstanding icon. Sincerely speaking, you are outstanding. Except you believe that you are, you may live the life of aren't. Living like you aren't disfigures the whole essence of your unique genetics. As a trained Biochemist, I can confidently tell you that you're a unique figure, based on numerous scientific proofs. So, as an icon, maintain your pole position of being number one figure in your calling, dream and vision. An icon is a figure; you are a figure!

A Portrait: a portrait is not just a painting, drawing or photograph; it is also a verbal picture or description. When you describe a man, you profile him. The description of an icon is superbly prolific because of his antecedents of excellence. You may not be known now, but there is a potential high profile hidden inside you. If only you will take a step to move towards that dream you've always had with your eyes wide open, you will, soonest be dining with those you've always admired. What you have within is enough to make you a portrait if you stop looking down on yourself. Run towards your goal; stop acting small. You are a portrait; an expensive one indeed.

A Likeness: it is obvious that a likeness is a resemblance, image, picture, representation or portrait; but it is also the tendency to be liked or, the state or fact of being liked. As an icon, those who speak ill of you don't have a choice but to like you. They speak ill most times, because they envy you. Those on the opposing side actually admire your skills and charisma; they don't admit it because you're scoring points to their own disadvantage. Anytime Arsenal Football Club plays against Manchester United, I am always praying for Manchester United to lose; not because I don't realise that some of their players are better than some players in my team, Arsenal. But because they're scoring at my disadvantage, I wouldn't like them to win. As an icon, something in you exhumes likeness; some people hate you because they see something likeable in you. If they can see it, why are you ignorant of who you are? You are an icon. See it; you're a likeness!

An Idol: the first impression in people's minds when the word idol is mentioned is evil. Idol does not only have an evil connotation but also means something good. The best definition of idol is someone that is revered, admired, or highly loved. Without reverence, admiration or love, you can't achieve much in your pursuits. To actualise a purpose, relationship is a key factor. You're an idol, not to be worshiped but to be respected and loved. You are respect personified; don't deny it. You are a bundle of love; don't reject it. You are a reverend even if you don't stand on the pulpit. You are simply an icon!

A Model: a model is a standard or example for comparison. It is the yardstick for measuring quality. You are a standard; you are a yardstick. As a standard, you must stand out. As a yardstick, you must measure up. Don't lag behind, because you are an icon.

WHAT ARE THE CHARACTERISTICS OF AN ICON?

Every icon has a distinguishing feature. Every icon has something that makes it unique. Uniqueness makes you stand out of the crowd; it puts you on a different platform, far from the rest. Therefore, some major characteristics of icons are:

Boldness: courage is an iconic identity. Fearlessness is an iconic feature. An icon must be daring. An icon must not be afraid of breaking the rules of propriety. To be an icon, you must be at the forefront. To be an icon, you must be impudent. Icons go beyond conventions; they go beyond the usual or standard limit; that is what makes them champions. Boldness characterises iconic nature.

Clarity and Visibility: without boldness, you can't possess clarity and visibility. In addition to boldness, positioning is a major key in visibility. If you're bold but not well positioned, you will be obscure. Icons are not just bold; they are clear and visible because they know how to position themselves. Any product that is clear and visible on the shelf was well positioned. As an icon, rightly position yourself so that you can be more impactful.

Attractiveness: anything that is attractive has a background of design and art; therefore, it has a defined structure, colour and beauty. An icon has a design and art, which makes it a beauty to behold. Beauty attracts. Beauty stands out. As an icon, you are a paragon of beauty. Your beauty is not defined by your physical shape or appearance; it is defined by who you are inside. If you let your inner being to reflect on the outer world, the world will see what a treasure you are. You've always been; only that you never realised it or admitted it. Your true self is attractive. Yes, you are!

Simplicity: icons are easy to understand and deal with. Icons are modest and uncomplicated. Icons are not deceitful, artificial, assuming, or pretentious. Be an icon!

Simplicity is the mother of genuine peace. Simplicity makes the world a better place to live in. Simplicity is life. Be an icon!

Touch-Ability: in modern day mobile or cell phones and electronic tablets, touch screens have become the new age technology. Most people, rather than click buttons on the phones to access certain applications, prefer to touch the icons in order to easily reach their intended destinations.

As an icon, you must be touchable. There are some people who consider themselves to be icons but are untouched by people's pains, feelings and desperate conditions. Some people live in palaces but don't care about those that live in carcasses. That is not the attitude of an icon. If you cannot be touched, you're a con, not an icon.

Accessibility: if I can't access you, I can't assess you. Some people are too high; they cannot be reached. Some people are too deep; they cannot be located, yet, they claim to be icons. If you can be touched but can't be accessed, you're just a figure-head icon. It can be so frustrating touching an icon on a tablet or phone, but can't access it. Accessibility is the proof to your workability. How do I know that you're functioning when you're not responding?

Possession of quality content and ability to effectively communicate it: on the screens of my computers, tablet and mobile phone are various icons. Each icon was designed to access a specific information or message. As you click an icon, it leads you into a world of information or content. A social media icon leads you into the world of networking. A television icon helps you access moving pictures. A radio icon makes you hear audio broadcast. So, every icon has content and kind of, effectively communicates that content.

One ill I've discovered in certain people is that they spend so much time designing icons that have little or no content. On the outside, they look wow, but when accessed, they are empty. Any icon that does not work on its content will be embarrassed when accessed. As an icon, you must endeavour to create quality contents. It is your content that defines your true identity. It is your content that reflects your genetics. If I access you, what will I find inside you? If I probe you, what can I get out of you? What you have inside is what you bring outside when you're stripped. Opportunities will strip you, so if you're empty, never seek opportunities because you'll be embarrassed. Challenges will strip you; be ready because purpose and vision are not always delicious.

Some people have quality contents but don't have enough communication skills to unleash it. No one can bring out of you, what you don't let them know you have. You must, as an icon, be able to say at least, what you have. What you don't say, no one can help to refine. So, build up your communication skills so that you can shine in the world. You are a light; don't hide under a bushel!

CHAPTER TWO

ORDINARY PEOPLE WITH EXTRAORDINARY MENTALITIES

Although, according to www.psychologytoday.com, the story below did not actually happen, but was adapted from Stephenson, G. R. (1967) social science research using rhesus monkeys, the relevance of this fictional research cannot be overlooked. This story is called the Monkey Banana and Water Spray Experiment.

The monkey banana and water spray experiment is a perfect example of describing not just the mentality of animals, but also that of man. In the experiment, 5 monkeys were locked inside a cage. A banana was hung on the ceiling while a ladder was placed underneath it. Immediately sighting the banana, one of the monkeys decided to climb the ladder in order to take it. As soon as he started climbing, the researcher, with a hose, sprayed ice-cold water on him, and in addition, sprayed the ice-cold water on the other 4 monkeys that didn't climb. When a second monkey attempted to climb the ladder, the researcher again, sprayed ice-cold water on the monkey in addition to the other 4 observing monkeys. This climb and spray was repeated over and over again until the monkeys learned their lessons. In their mentality, it was registered permanently that as far as the cage was concerned, climbing the ladder is equivalent to the inconvenience of being sprayed with ice-cold water.

When the researcher succeeded in stereotyping the mindset of the 5 monkeys, he substituted one of the monkeys with an inexperienced one. This new monkey was never aware of the ice-cold water, but the other 4 were. As expected, as soon as the new monkey came in, and saw the banana and the ladder, he decided to quickly have a go, but the other experienced monkeys pulled him down and beat him up, even if the researcher had stopped spraying ice-cold water. So, in the mentality of the new monkey, it was registered that climbing the ladder is synonymous to being beaten. One after the other, all the monkeys in the cage were substituted with inexperienced monkeys, yet, they all kept beating up the new monkeys that attempted climbing the ladder without any previous knowledge or experience of ice-cold water spray. None of the 4 new monkeys bothered asking why.

When the fifth monkey was introduced and was also beaten up, he turns with a curious face asking why he was being beaten while trying to get the banana. The other 4 were puzzled because they had no answer since they were never aware of the ice-cold water spray nor have they ever experienced it. In the same vein, men beat up other men that attempt to climb onto higher heights in life without knowing why they're doing it. Until he asks why, he will join the gang of stereotypes, beating those who intend to go up. Instead of beating the odds, some people beat men. To beat life, you must beat the odds. To beat the odds, you must have an extraordinary mentality.

There are people who have been beaten by life, systems and backgrounds, yet refused to give up. These people are ordinary people but with extraordinary mentalities. It takes extraordinary mentality to climb up to take what belongs to you. I have read of many who did not cowardly submit their meals to the odds of the day, but in this chapter, I've decided to mention just a few. Some of them are well known, while the others are unknown, but in spite of not being known, they are ICONS!

ICON 1: He was born 27 October 1945. He was the seventh of eight children. His parents were later divorced while his dad, in 1978 died of alcoholism. He got married in 1969 but in 1971, his pregnant wife died of hepatitis; the little boy in the womb was also lost. He had very little formal education; he only learnt to read when he was ten years old. He had to quit school after the second grade in order to work to help his family. He started working at the age of twelve as a shoe shiner and a street vendor. When he was fourteen years old, he got his first formal job in a copper processing factory as a lathe operator.

At age 19, he lost the little finger on his left hand in an accident while working as a press operator in an automobile parts factory. After losing his finger, he had to run to several hospitals before receiving medical attention. This experience increased his interest in participating within the Workers' Union. Around that time, he became involved in union activities and held several important union posts. This man ran for presidency in his country three times without success. He failed in 1989, 1994 and 1998, but in 2002, he became the president of Brazil. His name is *Luiz Inácio Lula da Silva.*

Luiz Inácio Lula da Silva is regarded as the most popular politician ever to come out of Brazil. While in office, he was one of the world's most popular leaders. He was featured in

Time's The 100 Most Influential People in the World for 2010. It may suffice you to know that Lula is also a cancer survivor. In spite of his pains, *Luiz Inácio Lula da Silva is an icon!*

ICON 2: Living on the edge of Nairobi National Park, he first became responsible for herding and safeguarding his family's cattle when he was nine years old. But often, his valuable livestock would be raided by the lions roaming the park's sweet savannah grasses, leaving him to count the losses. At the age of 11, he decided that it was time to find a way of protecting his family's cows, goats and sheep from falling prey to hungry lions. His light bulb moment came with one small observation. One day, while walking around, he discovered that lions were scared of moving lights.

He further noticed that lions were afraid of venturing near the farm's stockade when someone was walking around with a flashlight. He put his young mind to work and a few weeks later he'd come up with an innovative, simple and low-cost system to scare the predators away.

He fitted a series of flashing LED bulbs onto poles around the livestock enclosure, facing outward. The lights were wired to a box with switches and to an old car battery powered by a solar panel. They were designed to flicker on and off intermittently, thus tricking the lions into believing that someone was moving around carrying a flashlight. And it worked. Since he rigged up his "Lion Lights," his family has not lost any livestock to the wild beasts, to the great delight of his father and astonishment of his neighbors. What's even more impressive is that he devised and installed the whole system by himself, without ever receiving any training in electronics or engineering. The 13-year-old's remarkable ingenuity was recognized with an invitation to the TED 2013 conference, held in California, where he shared the stage with some of the world's greatest thinkers, innovators and scientists. His name is Richard Turere; a Maasai boy from the village called Kitengela, Kenya.

In spite of his humble background, colour and nationality, he is an icon.

ICON 3: She was born in Johannesburg on 4 March 1932. When she was eighteen days old, her mother was arrested for selling umqombothi; an African homemade beer. Her mother was sentenced to six months imprisonment. So, compulsorily, this woman spent her first six months of life in jail. At the age of six, she lost her father.

As a child, she sang in the choir of the Kilmerton Training Institute in Pretoria, a primary school that she attended for eight years. In 1950 at the age of eighteen, she gave birth to her only child, Bongi whose father was her first husband James Kubay. She was then diagnosed with breast cancer, and her husband left her shortly afterwards.

Her professional career began in the 1950s when she was featured in the South African jazz group; the Manhattan Brothers, and appeared for the first time on a poster. She left the Manhattan Brothers to record with her all-woman group, The Skylarks, singing a blend of jazz and traditional melodies of South Africa. As early as 1956, she released her single which was played on all the radio stations and made her name known throughout South Africa.

In the 1960s she was the first artist from Africa to popularize African music around the world. She recorded and toured with many popular artists, such as Harry Belafonte, Paul Simon, and Hugh Masekela.

She campaigned against the South African system of apartheid. The South African government responded by revoking her passport in 1960 and her citizenship and right of return in 1963. In spite of that, she never gave up on her beliefs, career and passion. In 1966, she received the Grammy Award for Best Folk Recording together with Harry Belafonte for An Evening with Belafonte/Makeba. Zenzile Miriam Makeba (4 March 1932-9 November 2008) popularly known for her song 'Pata Pata' was an icon.

ICON 4: He was born 13 September, 1969 in New Orleans, Louisiana. He was one of four children. He had a difficult childhood suffering years of abuse at the hands of his carpenter father. He once described his father as a man 'whose answer to everything was to beat it out of you'. At a point, he attempted suicide in order to escape the challenges at home. At the age of 16, he changed his first name as a way of distancing himself from his father. He dropped out of high school, but later earned a general equivalency diploma. Trying to find his way professionally, he held a series of unfulfilling jobs before discovering his true passion.

One day, while watching an episode of Oprah Winfrey Show, he was inspired by a comment on the program about how writing about difficult experiences could lead to personal breakthroughs. He started a series of letters to himself, which became the basis for the musical, 'I Know I've Been Changed'. After saving up $12,000, he debuted the show—which he directed, produced, and starred in—at an Atlanta theatre in 1992. The musical's run lasted only one weekend and drew a measly 30 people to see the show.

Disappointed yet determined, he continued to work odd jobs while reworking the show. He staged the show in several other cities, but success still eluded him. Broke, he was living and sleeping in his car for a time. In 1998, he tried one more time to win over theatre audiences. He rented out the House of Blues in Atlanta for another production of 'I Know I've Been Changed'. Soon, he was performing to sell out crowds and the musical was moved to a larger theatre. After so many years of hard work, he finally earned critical acclaim as well as commercial success.

His name is Tyler Perry born as Emmitt Perry Jr; the multimillionaire writer, actor, producer, director, entrepreneur, and academy award winner. Tyler has won numerous awards as a film actor, filmmaker, playwright, and screenwriter.

ICON 5: He was born on 1 October, 1966 in the slums of Monrovia, Liberia. He grew up in one of the city's worst slums called Clara Town. He was raised by his grandmother after his parents split off. Fortunately, he developed into a tall, athletic teenager, and began playing soccer for the Young Survivors youth club at 15. He moved on to other prominent local clubs as his skills progressed, assuming starring roles for Mighty Barrolle and Invincible Eleven.

At 22, he was discovered by then, Cameroon national team coach Claude Le Roy, who relayed news of his abilities to AS Monaco manager Arsène Wenger. Wenger flew to Africa to get a look for himself, and then signed him to his club. He played for different top football clubs in Europe including AC Milan. In 1995, he won the FIFA World Player of the Year; the world's topmost football award in spite of the fact that he never played in a world cup competition.

His name is George Tawlon Manneh Oppong Ousman Weah, popularly known as George Weah. Liberia was war torn, but George Weah wasn't because he had the mentality to beat the odds. Apart from winning FIFA best footballer, he was a runner-up in 1996. He also won various awards such as European best footballer, African best footballer, various football leagues awards, FA cups, and much more. In 2005, although was unsuccessful, he contested the Liberian presidential election. George was one of the most successful black footballers ever to come out of this world. He is an icon; a great icon indeed.

ICON 6: It happened on one unforgettable day. He was just fourteen years old. He lit a candle, and slept off but little did he know that the burning candle would drop on the rug. He only woke up and realised that the house was on fire when his arm started burning. He got up in the middle of a blazing flame; the whole house was so hot and felt like a furnace. While in the flame, he started shouting for help. Suddenly, he heard a voice from one of his neighbours encouraging him to hold on, and letting him know that the ambulance and fire engine were on their way. After about 10 minutes of waiting, he couldn't bear the intense heat anymore, so he made a decision to jump down from the third floor of the building. He did, and landed on the concrete floor. The only thing he could remember was that oxygen mask was fixed on his face. He had a 35% degree burn, and spent six months in the hospital. Apart from his face, the rest of his body were completely scarred. His friends nicknamed him SCAR. As a result of his physical appearance, he completely lost his self esteem. Due to this, he lost focus in school, and failed his O' level English Language examination four times.

Whenever his peers wrote in class, he would never take the chance to write because he felt insecure. In his mind, he would imagine everyone staring at his scarred hands, so, he refused to use the hands. Outside school, he hung around people that took him further away from his positive dreams. In order to feel accepted, he joined a gang that introduced him to cannabis and prodigal living. He began losing his memory. He lost everything, and it was hard for him to believe in his abilities. He didn't have anyone to encourage him since his parents were separated, and his siblings were busy doing their own things. One day, while on the bus, he met a young lady he admired so much. Sooner than later, they started dating, but this didn't last long. She was more interested in the gifts she was receiving from him, since that was the only way he felt he could buy love.

They finally parted when she gained admission into the University. After several attempts to win her back failed, he made a decision to pursue life with a purpose. His failed relationship became an eye opener. He turned his disappointment and anger to passion. His dream to go to the University rekindled. He rewrote his O' Level English Language examination, and passed. After that, he applied to University of Greenwich, London. In 2009, he graduated with a First Class Honours degree in Biomedical Sciences. This ordinary person with extraordinary mentality is called Deji Yusuf. Apart from working as a Biomedical Scientist, he is a motivational speaker and the author of the book, 'How to Live Your Dreams'. Take it or leave it, Deji's life is an inspiration. Believe it or not, Deji is an icon!

ICON 7: He was born 13 May, 1950 in Saginaw, Michigan. He was the third of six children. As a result of being born six weeks premature, the blood vessels at the back of his eyes had not yet reached the front and their aborted growth caused the retina to detach thereby making him experience the condition known as retinopathy of prematurity. This condition was escalated by the excessive oxygen in his incubator as a premature baby. Due to this circumstance, he was born blind.

When he was four, his mother left his father and moved to Detroit with her children. She later changed his surname. At a tender age, his musical skills began to manifest. He became a multi-instrumentalist and was active in his church choir. He was just 11 years old when he was discovered by Ronnie

White of The Miracles; a Motown Band. In late 1961, his first record was released. This man was born with the name Steveland Hardaway Judkins; his mother renamed him Steveland Hardaway Morris, but the whole world know him as Stevie Wonder.

Stevie Wonder is a multiple Grammy Award Winner and one of the most celebrated singers the earth has ever had. Stevie Wonder is an icon; a big one indeed. He never made excuses for his condition, but went ahead to pursue his vision. He had an extraordinary mentality, though from an ordinary background with extraordinary challenges. If he had made excuses, the world would have understood, but he never. Today, Stevie Wonder is a household name all over the world.

ICON 8: Dr. Devi Prasad Shetty was born 8 May, 1953. He was born in Kinnigoli, South Canara District, Karnataka, India. He was the eight of nine children. His desire to become a heart surgeon was aroused in his fifth grade when he heard of a South African surgeon that performed the world's first heart transplant. After completing his graduate degree in Medicine and post-graduate work in General Surgery from Kasturba Medical College, Mangalore, he trained in cardiac surgery at Guy's Hospital in the United Kingdom. He returned to India in 1989 and initially worked at B.M. Birla Hospital in Kolkata. He performed the first neonatal heart surgery in the country on a 9-day-old baby. In Kolkata he operated on Mother Theresa after she had a heart attack and subsequently served as her personal physician. After some time, he moved to Bangalore and started the Manipal Heart Foundation at Manipal Hospital, Bangalore. Financial contribution for the construction of the hospital was provided by Dr. Shetty's father-in-law.

In the year 2000, he started Narayana Hrudayalaya Hospital in Bangalore. Narayana Hrudayalaya means 'Temple of the heart'. India has a population of about 1.2 billion people, with about 40% living below the poverty level. For the 40 percent of those people who live below the poverty line, getting good quality healthcare is difficult and often impossible. A serious illness or accident in a family can cripple their finances and affect the prospects of generations to come. Borrowing money or selling assets for medical needs is the most common reason for indebtedness in India. Yet, under the guidance of Dr Devi Shetty, cardiac surgeon, innovative businessman and founder, the Narayana Hrudayalaya hospital is addressing some of these inequalities and inequities.

The hospital provides the most complex operations on an industrial scale. And it needs to as India is a country where two million cardiac operations are needed every year, but only 95,000 are carried out. In Narayana Hrudayalaya Hospital, paediatric open heart surgeries are undertaken each year than anywhere else in the world. Up to 500 cataract operations are performed per day. Cardiac surgery costing $40,000 to $50,000 or more in the US has a baseline cost here of just $1,800. Its huge scale and improved efficiencies allow the hospital to reduce costs, not only for those who can afford to pay, but also for the very poor who can get the best care the hospital can offer at virtually no cost through assistance from the hospital's charity unit. Yet, the hospital makes nine percent profit per annum, while operating a policy of never sending away patients who cannot afford treatment, and retaining world-class standards of healthcare. Some see the hospital as a possible role model for Western health providers who are struggling with the burden of providing excellence in healthcare on an affordable scale.

Dr. Devi Prasad Shetty is a multiple award winner in the field of medicine and entrepreneurship. He is referred to, as the Henry Ford of healthcare. Devi Shetty is a man with the interest of the ordinary man at heart. He doesn't just live for himself, but also lives for the common poor man in the street. Devi Shetty is an icon. He may not be a celebrity to the world, but he is, to the lives he has saved. Devi Shetty; an ordinary man with an extraordinary mentality!

ICON 9: According to United Nations, about 10,000 child soldiers were used in Sierra Leone's civil war. Till date, after the war, most of these children wallow in the streets jobless and without access to quality education. As a result, they have become targets for greedy politicians who use them to cause trouble in the society as a way of settling their scores with fellow politicians. Most of the political violence in Sierra Leone is perpetrated by majority of these ex-combatant child soldiers. In the midst of all these, a teenage boy, in spite of being seriously under-privileged decided to make a difference.

Kelvin Doe was born in 1997 to a poor family in a poor community in Sierra Leone. Despite his humble background, he deliberately refused to be pinned down by the ugly claws of poverty and deprivation. Kelvin, with his inventive mind has done what most kids in the western world with all its western education and exposure couldn't do. He has built his own battery out of acid, soda, and metal parts scavenged from trash bins that he now uses to light up area homes in his community. He has also built a homemade FM radio transmitter plus a generator to power it. These, he uses to run his own community radio station. Due to his innovative skills, he was invited to spend a few weeks in MIT Media Lab in United States, where he worked alongside graduate students. During his visit to the U.S, he was granted access to MIT's resources and mentors. He even met with Harvard University president.

When most kids all over Sierra Leone, Africa and the entire world make excuses why they can't standout, Kelvin Doe, chose the positive alternative. DJ Focus, as he's popularly known on his radio station decided to live his dream by being focused. According to him, his next project is to build a windmill. Who on earth would debate it, that Kelvin is an ordinary boy in the street with an extraordinary mentality? I don't think any purposeful mind would do that!

ICON 10: Some people are born into wealthy families, but most of them end up having un-wealthy mentalities. This conclusion is drawn from the fact that, when most wealthy people die, their children are unable to either maintain the tempo of their wealth or multiply it. Some children, not just born with silver but gold spoons have rapidly depreciated the assets entrusted to them rather than appreciate them. As a result, it is generally believed that wealthy children are spoilt children. But this was not the case with Aliko Dangote; Africa's wealthiest man.

Aliko Dangote was born in Kano, Nigeria on 10 April, 1957. His mother was the granddaughter of a wealthy businessman known as Dantata while his father was Dantata's business associate. In 1977 after graduating from the University, his uncle loaned him half a million of Nigeria's currency; it was a business loan. This was at the age of 21. With the money, he began a trading firm. As a visionary, he wasn't satisfied with trading alone, but had processing and manufacturing in mind. With prudence, excellent leadership and focus, he ventured into food processing, cement manufacturing and freight. His ability to generate cutting edge creative and innovative ideas helped build his business. Today, his business employs over 11,000 people. He was rated by Forbes as Africa's wealthiest man.

Aliko Dangote; an entrepreneur with a heart of flesh, philanthropist and a strategic leader is an ordinary man with an extraordinary mentality. In a continent where most wealthy people prefer to stack their money abroad, sit back and watch common people in the streets die, Dangote expands his organisations in order to offer more employment opportunities to ordinary people. Through the salaries and wages earned by these employees, they're able to send their children to school and also provide for their families. Take it or leave it, Aliko Dangote is an icon.

The world has produced many icons; you too can be one. You have what it takes; yes, you do. You are a potential icon!

CHAPTER THREE

CHANGE THAT MINDSET

The number one attribute every icon has is a changed mindset. Icons think out of the box. To be an icon, you must have a changed mindset. If you keep reasoning like the man of yesterday, you can't live a successful life, tomorrow. Too unfortunate, many are still stuck in the box because they have defeatist mindset. Yet, the same people want to be icons in their world. It is not possible to have an old skin, and expect a new wine to be poured into it. If you want new wine, change your bottle. If you don't have a bottle, change your can. Whatever container you have must be new in order to receive something new. Renew your mind so that you can behold a new vision.

On the road to the positive vision you see in your mind, are many potholes. These potholes most often stop many people from striving for the creative imaginations in their hearts. Because of the strains, many give up to settle for what most people settle for; the base of the pyramid. This base is full and thick; so condensed that there is so much war there, because there's hardly any fresh air to breath. In spite of the battles within, many prefer to relish in it with self pity as the only consolation that keeps them going, daily. A few, who see the picture with determination, fight; though it may take ages, but their resilience brings them out of the pestilence.

Long before writing this book, even as a growing child, I made up my mind that being at the bottom of life is not prestige. I saw many people within my inner circle not make moves to step out of where they perceive life has kept them. I knew as a child that if a man strives, he can reach any height. Although life attempted to batter me, so that I can give up my believes, I have kept the faith; the faith that it doesn't have to be in my time, to reap all the benefits of someone who kept his push despite the odds that were too hard to beat. I considered myself a foundation of an empire not yet seen, whose walls will be built by the seeds that will come after him; my children, grandchildren, and beyond.

While waiting for change to happen as I daily sat on my little table in the kitchen to write articles and books meant to encourage people to make the right decisions in life, cash was a major problem. The system affected my cash flow, and this in turn had a painful impact on my family and vision. In order to get out of this sinking ship, I made a decision to do any job that will at least, keep my family going while I continue working on the future. Flexibility has always been my game; I know that every situation encountered must be tackled with wisdom in order to overcome the challenges that are posed. So, I got a cleaning job.

On certain weekends, I'll be called by my supervisor regarding some offices or kitchens that needed to be cleaned in and out of London. He would pick us up with the company van in a certain part of the city en route our destination. At first, I was bitter about my situation, and would mutter words like, 'Ken, you shouldn't be here. What are you doing here? Why is life treating you like a beggar?' I couldn't leave because I had a family to look after. Later on, rather than get bitter, I began to ask myself some more goal oriented questions. I understand that every scene in life creates an opportunity for change;

you either get changed or become the change. This change in mindset made me re-evaluate my reason for doing the kind of job and hanging out with the type of people. So, one day, I said to myself, 'what is my purpose in this place?' The word, purpose triggered something in me because I believe that good or bad, there is a reason for being where you are; that reason produces an assignment for you to do.

Anytime we travelled together to the different places to do our cleaning jobs, there was always one topic or the other meant for discussion. My observation was that most of these topics were centred on self limiting beliefs; the belief that the colour of your skin can affect your success level was a major point I kept hearing from my folks a lot of times. At first, I played down the impact of what this discussion may either have on me, or already had on my dear friends. One day before going to work, I laid on the bed to ponder. With a bit of understanding, I know the power of words; especially what you hear daily. I knew that if I don't rise up to superimpose my positive beliefs on my friends, I will either start thinking like them or not doing them any good with my concurring attitude. On this awesome day, when the topic was again raised, I vehemently disagreed with them, and gave them many infallible reasons why they need a change of mindset. I talked about the impact it will have on their children if they don't change the way they think. I made them believe that what you think and say consciously or unconsciously create your environment, and that you end up becoming your environment. On that day, there was a huge debate all day long, but I succeeded in making them see reasons with me.

After the heated debate, the phrase, Change That Mindset just wouldn't leave my mind. It began to dawn on me that most people have problems dealing with their mindsets in various facets of life. In personal lives, entrepreneurship, relationship, professionalism, education, and even much more, the mindsets of people have debarred them from scoring high points in their pursuits. On that day, I began to consider writing a piece on this subject. Though I felt that many books are available on the topic, but everyone has his approach; various approaches meet various needs. I believe that my reason for coming in contact with my lovely friends was to birth this chapter; Change That Mindset!

On another occasion, at Charring Cross, London, as a member of a team working for a market research company, we were recruiting people on the street to take part in a survey being conducted in a popular hotel within the environ. Suddenly, a man walked up to me and asked, 'what are you guys doing?' I told him, and asked if he was interested, as there was incentive for participating. He said, 'I am not interested', and followed the statement with, 'I have stopped working long ago. I deliberately sat at home so that I can rip off the benefits system. You guys that are working are stupid. If you go on the benefits system, you'll make more money'. When he finished making his statement, he didn't wait for me to respond before zooming off into the street.

I considered his stupidity and how much he is cheating himself, and I pitied his ignorance. In his awkward imagination, he has established a mindset that barricades him from reaching his best potentials. In his mind, he thinks he's cheating the government but the main person he's cheating is himself! As a man full of energy, working to make a living opens massive doors of opportunities for him to showcase his talents, make better money and become more useful to his world. By this, he leaves a legacy of success for those coming behind him, and a good name for the generations to come. The mindset of man is what stops him; the mentality of man is what prevents him from making a meaning headway in life.

What is Mindset?

Mindset, because of its total involvement in the behaviour of man, has diverse definitions, but all coming to one meaning when interpreted. According to Online Etymology Dictionary, it appears like the word was first used in the 1920s as slang. Then, it simply meant 'habits of mind formed by previous experience'. Today, as civilisation brings more opportunities for interactions, the definition is getting wider. Let us take a look at how other dictionaries define mindset in order to give us a broader understanding. For instance, Wikipedia defines it as 'in decision theory and general systems theory, a mindset is a set of assumptions, methods, or notations held by one or more people or groups of people that is so established that it creates a powerful incentive within these people or groups to continue to adopt or accept prior behaviors, choices, or tools'. Collins Dictionary goes ahead to say that mindset is 'the ideas and attitudes with which a person approaches a situation, especially when these are seen as being difficult to alter'. With a further look into the Oxford Dictionary, it was defined as 'the established set of attitudes held by someone'. Simply put, in Cambridge Dictionary's opinion, mindset is 'a person's way of thinking and their opinions' while Encarta Dictionary says a mindset is 'a set of beliefs or a way of thinking that determine somebody's behaviour and outlook'.

From the above definitions, it is obvious that there are certain factors that affect the mindset of man. I will take some of these factors one after the other, to explain how they impact a person's lifestyle.

Habits: I have a very good friend whose habit is talking loud even when sitting in a public place. One day, while on the train with her, she began her usual loud conversation. I said to her, 'can you keep your voice down a bit. Other people are listening to our conversation'. She said, 'Ken, please leave me alone. It's my nature. That's the way I talk'. Then I said, 'if that's the way you talk, say with a loud voice, "I am a prostitute!"' She started laughing because she knew she couldn't say that. Her sanity was restored when she realised that in spite of her habit, her mindset can be changed when certain issues arise.

Many people are chained by certain habits because over the years, they have consciously or unconsciously imbibed certain characters that aren't in their own interest. When corrected, they become defensive and emotional, and then look for the best sympathetic excuse to make in order for their habits to be accepted as norm. Habits form the mindset of man. Sometimes, these mindsets are retrogressive, but the people that have cultivated those habits over the years don't see anything wrong with them, so they carry on until it either maims them, or somehow, someone points it out to them. Those with teachable spirits and willing to change seek solutions to correct their anomalies, but others just maintain the set. Wrong habits produce wrong mindsets, and wrong mindsets produce wrong outcomes!

Experiences: Some stories you hear take you into the way many people reason. Sometimes, you wonder if these stories are true. Once, I was told a story by one woman that gave me her reason for getting married a bit late. She said that her dad tortured her mum by physically abusing and assaulting her for so many years. As a child, she witnessed these evils meted out by her father. So, she made a decision never to get married. At that point, no man was emotionally attracted to her. It took a lot of intervention to change her mindset. When she finally got married, her sexual life was affected, because in spite of the fact that she loves her husband, she felt no sexual urge for him. That became another issue that needed to be dealt with until she overcame it. She's lucky to have overcome it because some people never.

36

Many people's previous experiences affect their mindsets, and make it difficult for them to move on in life. Until they decisively embrace change, nothing will change. It is up to the person with an experience to stop looking back to the days of hurts, and look forward to the future full of hope and love.

Not all experiences that affect the mindset appear to be negative. There are some that mean no harm but may actually be harmful or make a person stagnant. Take for instance, an introvert. One experience or the other may have put him in that position or maybe, his parents were not sensitive enough to help him enhance his interpersonal skills as a child. One way or the other, experience may have played a role in his current mindset.

Culture: In my opinion, culture is the major determinant of mindset. It is the behaviours and beliefs characteristic of a particular social, ethnic, or age group. Let us take a brief look at the social culture of binge drinking. In certain mindsets, it's been established that a night out is equivalent to a night of alcohol consumption. For such people, if alcohol isn't involved, they haven't had a good night. In order to make their night out worthwhile, they drink themselves to stupor and become social menace. For a society with national insurance policies, these types of people become burdens to other contributors because of their mindsets.

Another branch of cultural mindset is racism. It is insanity to have a racial mindset. How can a man who loves his black shoes suddenly hate a black colour when he sees it on the skin of another man? How can a woman who loves her white blouse become hateful when she sees a white person? It doesn't make sense; insanity is senseless!

Forced marriage for instance is as a result of cultural mindset. Some parents believe that in an internet broadband age, a son or daughter must marry from their ethnic group. Without further ado, I must agree that some truths cannot be changed, but not in deciding the ethnicity of a spouse. The choice of where to marry is the sole responsibility of the person involved in the marriage, not the parents. Some cultural mindsets split the world into unholy multiples.

Sometimes, I wonder why some decades ago, in a certain part of the world, giving birth to twins was considered evil. In that culture, as at then, twins were killed until a missionary came to change their mindsets.

The Gangsterism on our streets today is due to some youthful mindsets. The young people have so much energy, so they take it out on themselves. There is this thinking among many young people that to prove that you're strong and bold, you must do something stupid. So they pick up weapons and waste valuable lives; they punctuate the destinies of fellow young people that would have become assets in the near future. Some youth cultures produce bad mindsets.

Assumption: Assumption always concludes that a certain method of approach should be the way things must be done. A preacher once told the story of a woman who always sliced off the edges of pancakes after frying. When asked her reason for doing so, she said that her mother taught her to, and therefore, that is the norm. When her mother was asked her reason for slicing off the edges of pancakes after frying, she said because their fry pan was too small, so, she had to chop off the excess bits that didn't fit into the pan. Without asking questions, her daughter made an assumption and developed a mindset in that direction.

Assumption takes things for granted by making presumptions that are merely hypothetical without verifying the facts. Assumptions have ruined some good relationships because one or two people involved postulated theories that weren't real, therefore, it crashed the footpath bridging the gap in a harmonious relationship. People who constantly make assumptions about others develop unhealthy mindsets. If these mindsets aren't promptly dealt with, it ends up damaging the people involved.

Beliefs: Beliefs are sometimes, personal. No matter how much you inject knowledge into people, if they have their personal beliefs; it becomes difficult to change them. Some people, for instance, have the belief that Mathematics is difficult. The moment they see figures and symbols, they start panicking. For such people, simply scribble the symbol > on paper, and they will start breaking sweat. The symbol > means greater than, but the mindset that Mathematics is difficult makes a person conclude that the symbol > means some strange things beyond greater than.

Beliefs form the lifestyles of individuals, decision making processes and their conclusions about how things are or should be. A person's opinion, right or wrong, shapes his mindset. The mindset in turn affects the person's successes or failures in a specific dimension. Except a negative belief is appropriately tackled, the person involved might be chained in the garrison of retrogression for life. For instance, I have a cousin that once told me, 'I will make sure that my first son goes through some severe hardship in life because when a child undergoes serious challenges, he becomes wiser and better'. Wherever he got that opinion from, I can't tell, but what I know is that his belief is erratic, and might spell doom for his son. So many people come up with some funny but serious line of thoughts that doesn't just affect them but many connected to them. May I hastily point out that secular education does not eradicate backward beliefs; sometimes, it reinforces it. I have seen professors that are tied down by funny

39

ideologies that don't make sense. I have seen some top career and professional people that are hoodwinked by their personal idiosyncrasies. Tackling negative beliefs start from self realisation and making move for transformation.

Thoughts and Imaginations: Thoughts are words; imaginations are pictures. One of my favourite quotes in the Bible is 'As he thinketh, so is he'. This means that a man is the exact personality of what he thinks. In summary, I would say, 'man is thoughts personified'. The actions taken by man are enforced by his thoughts. The decisions made by man are engineered by his thoughts. Man's conclusions are dictated by his thoughts. The mindset of man is structured by thoughts.

When I hear on the News certain crimes committed by certain people, I usually ponder on what must have gone on in their minds. What you keep hearing affects what you keep thinking; what you keep thinking becomes what you keep doing. What you keep thinking and doing is sincerely, your mindset.

Imaginations are worse than thoughts because they are responsible for reinforcing thoughts. If you hear a word, you may forget, but if you see a picture, it is difficult for you to forget. That is the danger of watching pornographic movies. The pictures you've seen keep replaying on your mind, and those pictures come up with some thoughts, while the thoughts inspire you to act accordingly. Some of these people, if they don't have appropriate places to unleash their imaginations, commit rapes, and then, end up in jail. The same thing happens to those that have addiction for violent movies; some of these people end up in crimes.

Thoughts and imaginations shape the mindset of man. If he's not careful what he thinks, he'll think wrong and end up wrong.

What does Set do to the Mind?

Set makes the mind rigid: a rigid mind is a fixed, unyielding and inflexible mind. Rigidity hardly acknowledges the need for change.

There was the story of a man that relocated from Republic of Congo to Rwanda. He lived in Rwanda for over forty years; gave birth to all his children there, but couldn't understand the language. While in court one day, the daughter had to translate for him. His daughter told me that her father forbade them from learning the language and almost withdrew them from school because according to him, he is a typical Congolese, and the only languages he must speak are his native Congolese language and French. His rigidity affected his progress in a land that he should have flourished. The daughter on the other hand, learnt lessons from her father's rigidity and became flexible in her thinking. Today, she's a multi-linguist. In her profession as a Nurse, she's been able to help a lot of people that don't understand English find their directions in life through freelance mentoring in the City of London.

Life has different platforms; you may be flexible on one platform but rigid on another. Find out where you're rigid but requires flexibility, and work on it. Some people's rigidity may be found in the area of interpersonal relationship; if that's yours, deal with it. For others, it may be something else. Whatever it may be, you have the power to work on your mind. It belongs to you; you should be in control.

Set makes the mind bend: set inclines the mentality of a man by forcing it from a straight form to an angular or curved one. For example, it is universally acceptable that a blue cup is a blue cup, but there are certain people you'll ask, 'what is the colour of this cup?' You'll be shocked when they tell you that it looks white, even if they don't suffer from colour blindness.

I remember going for a training programme with one of my former colleagues to another country, and I shared a room with him. The management of the guest house we stayed usually picked up our clothes to dry clean. One day, they brought our clothes and asked my roommate, 'are these yours?' Both of us knew the clothes were his, but rather than say, 'yes, they're mine', he took a closer look and said, 'maybe'. I was infuriated because that has always been his attitude. He never goes straight, and as a result wastes a lot of time over jobs that shouldn't take time, all because of his mindset.

When a mind sets, it strays into horrendous directions, assumes a bent posture and bows in submission to a defined way of reasoning in spite of its wrongness. Be sensitive; work on your mind; change your mindset.

Set makes the mind tightened: when a bolt is screwed, it gets tightened, but there are occasions that a bolt has been over-tightened to the extent that if you try to loose it, it becomes difficult to unscrew. In that position, if you try forcing the bolt to loosen, it gets worn out. A worn out bolt cannot be reused.

On issues and subjects, some set has tightened the minds of some people that it becomes difficult for them to reason and see things the way they actually are. No matter how much you put the facts before them, they are so tight that they cannot change their opinions and beliefs. If you force them, they get worn out. Anyone that is over-tightened in his opinion and beliefs cannot be corrected; if you try correcting them, they loose it by force. People who loose it by force have volatile attitudes; they are potential explosives that have the tendency to cause earthquakes in their environments.

Hiring an employee with a tightened mindset is danger to an organisation because they come up with their funny and one method ideologies that hardly make sense. Employees with tightened mindsets hardly adapt to strategic changes, and are sparingly innovative.

Can you help a person with an over-tightened mindset? I think it may be possible. If over-tightened bolts can be gently loosed through the process of lubrication, I believe the human mind can be transformed using the same strategy.

Set Makes the Mind Curdle: when cow milk is coagulated, curds are formed; curds make up the cheese that we eat. Milks therefore, can be pasteurised to make cheese, but I'm not aware of cheese being used to make milk. That is the danger of set making the mind curdle.

A mind that has been left to sour for a long time results in curdles. For example, in a relationship, people involved should mind what they say to each other when they have differences. And if any has uttered a negative or damaging word, apology should follow immediately because words are like seeds; the mind is the soil. If a negative utterance is left on the mind un-dealt with, it can reshape it through the process of curdling. A curdle, left for a long time can cause unforeseen damage to a relationship. Issues that happened for over twenty years have separated, perceivably, happy couples because curdles were formed in the mind.

Set Makes the Mind Stiff: have you ever had a stiff neck? You can recall how painful it was. The mind can also be stiff; when it does, it causes excruciating pains. The most regrettable aspect of a stiff mind is that it causes pains to the person involved and to everyone around. If you have a boss with a stiff mind, you'll daily go to work unhappy because

43

you can guess what your day will look like. If you have a business partner with a stiff mind, your progress is slowed down. If you have a spouse with a stiff mind, you feel better when you're not at home.

Stiffness doesn't make things move or work. Stiffness is comparable to a dead body; devoid of life. Set makes a mind stiff.

Set Makes the Mind Frame: a frame is what it is because it has a defined, specific and rigid structure. Imagine the window frame in your sitting room? Can you easily change its shape? Of course, no! To change the shape of your sitting room window requires a lot of work and expenses.

A mind that is wrongly framed is expensive to change, even if the person is willing. Bad frames create unfair borders; badly framed minds also create unfair borders for themselves, and for those around them.

There are framed minds of self centredness; for these people, anyone that dares into their territories to compete with their ambitions is a dead man. They may not kill with physical swords; but the manner of unhealthy competition they exhibit is more than the fiery bullet from the muzzle of a gun.

The most sympathetic framing of the mind is a person that was wrongly framed, not by his own making, but through other people's erroneous assumptions. Some people have been sent to jail for crimes they never committed because someone framed them up. The serious part of being innocent in a frame is that it gets into the mind of the person, and sometimes, into the subconscious. Some people that were wrongly framed never recovered after their release from jail. Some of them have deteriorated into mental depression. A bad or wrong frame is evil, especially when it affects the mind.

Set makes the mind stamped: a stamp is as a result of a forceful impression. Some impressions come in form of strong opinions that cannot be easily changed. It is comparable to a postage stamp, that when stuck on an envelope cannot be removed by a boisterous wind.

Some impressions are made by inks; others are made by heat. Whether ink or heat, some impressions cannot be easily erased. Inscribing a logo on a metal plate is made mostly by hot metal pencils. These hot metal sharp pointed ends bore themselves through the depth of the vessels, and then forcefully inscribe the words or symbols of intent. For life, these words or symbols remain.

In the same vein, on the minds of some people, certain patterns of lifestyles, beliefs or opinions have been inscribed; right or wrong, they just carry on with it.

Can impressions on the minds of people be changed? It appears very difficult to, but my conclusion is that on earth, nothing is impossible.

The Mediocre Mindset

A few years back, I had a discussion with a postgraduate student that was a close friend. During our discussion, I emphasised the relevance of a student not targeting an average result but pushing himself to perform extraordinarily. As I spoke, he started laughing, and said, 'you're just nailing me on the wall because what you mentioned is my typical mindset'.

I wouldn't say that I was the best of students while in school, but I didn't know what I now know. For those that have the opportunity to know beforehand, they have no excuse not to stand out.

Mediocrity is not all about academics; it envelops every aspect of our lives. There are mediocre businessmen and businesswomen. There are mediocre fathers and mothers, who can't take proper care of their children. There are also, mediocre leaders, who may have had first class in the Universities, but can't even manage themselves, let alone, other people. We can go on and on.

When mediocrity becomes a lifestyle, it affects the self esteem of a person. If an average minded person for instance, enters certain environments, he believes straightaway that everyone there is better than him, without knowing who they are.

The Social Services was invited by a school to help a six year old child get out of her shell because no matter how much the teacher tried, her level of withdrawal from the rest of the pupils was immense. On taking a closer look, her problem was from home. At home, mum and dad believed in average; walked and worked in average. Unconsciously, this belief system was imparted into the little princess; so, she began manifesting the symptom of believing that she can't do better than mediocrity. And this, adversely affected her performance in interpersonal skills. For weeks and months, the child was put on social therapy to help disabuse what was imputed into her by her parents.

When we imbibe mediocrity, it infects and affects people around us consciously or unconsciously. It-doesn't-matter mentality is mediocre mentality. I-have-done-my-best mentality is mediocre mentality because sometimes, what we call 'best' isn't actually the best. You hear certain people say, 'I can't kill myself. After all, I have done my best' When you probe further, you discover that most people that make such statements are not ready to push beyond their limits to get what will change them for good. Except you're ready to go extra miles to achieve your dream, you may never achieve it. Anyone that made it happen, didn't do it on a comfortable mattress; they slept on rocks and swam in freezing streams before they were able to cross over the barriers of limitation. To reach your enviable expectation, you must eschew mediocrity; otherwise, you may remain at your starting point forever.

Who is a Mediocre?

A mediocre is a person that has only ordinary mentality: anything ordinary is common. Anything common can easily be replaced. There are lots of jobs that are common; you don't require any special skill to do them, therefore, any idiot can do them. If an idiot can perform the tasks, why should you expect a good pay from it? If an idiot can play the role, why should you expect it to have job security? Okay, let us take it a bit further. Let us assume that you work in a profession that requires high skills. If in spite of your professional skills, your work ethics is dismal, you are nothing more than a mediocre. The treatment that will be meted to you will be equivalent to that handed over to a man without skills because you're not optimising your talent.

An only ordinary mentality has no depth and shows no depth in pursuits. Anything on the surface level is cheap; anything on the periphery of life is easy to obtain, and so, shouldn't be highly priced. The deeper the position of a treasure in the earth, the more useful and costly it is. Mediocrity is cheap; everyone, with little effort can attain it. It is not big news to obtain an average result; it is, when you are distantly outstanding!

A mediocre is a person with neither good nor bad mentality: lukewarm is a neither good nor bad mentality. A person that is neither good nor bad cannot be trusted because he has the ability to quickly slip into bad since he's one foot away from being bad. Scoring 50% in life can't take you anywhere; it will leave you in a position of spectators. If you go to the stadium to watch a football match, it will truly

47

dawn on you that spectators are the chief noise-makers. They can score a trillion goals from their seats, but if given the opportunity to kick the ball, cannot perform. The other sad thing about spectators is that they foot the bills of those playing. How do football clubs make their money? Of course, they make it from the spectators. You may argue that most of their income come from TV rights, but please understand that there are other forms of spectators, who don't sit in stadiums, but have theirs in form of television screens. Whether in the literal stadium or metaphorical one, spectators foot the bills.

If you are a performer, get on the stage. If you're unique, prove it. Your mentality will be tested when you move out of the midst of those who just talk without taking a single step to convert their words to substance. Step out of neither good nor bad mentality because it's taking you nowhere. If you want the world to hear from you, move away from the party of those that give ovation; be the one receiving the ovation.

A mediocre is a person with a barely adequate mentality: something that is barely adequate is something that is hardly enough. For some people, everything is barely adequate:

- Money; barely adequate
- Knowledge; barely adequate
- Food; barely adequate
- Education; barely adequate
- Talent; barely adequate
- Shelter; barely adequate
- Relationship; barely adequate
- Ideas; barely adequate
- Time; barely adequate

People with barely adequate attitude hardly have time for things of value. Some people are roaming the streets, doing nothing, but if you ask them to do an hour job for you, so that you give them $8, they tell you that they don't have time.

When I was a market research interviewer, we usually stopped people in the streets to take part in surveys. Most times, the respondents will be given about $7 for filling out maybe, a 25 minute questionnaire. Most of the people that refuse taking part in the surveys are those on the social benefit system. They don't work; they collect free money from the government, but still tell you that they've got no time. What are they doing with their time? Absolutely nothing! Their problem is a barely adequate mentality!!

Barely adequate mentality is truly mediocre mentality. If in the true sense, you always have things that are barely adequate, you must fight your way out of that position. Never accept a situation that puts you in the bottom of life. Never conclude that that is how you were born to be. No one was deliberately born to suffer; don't accept that philosophy even if it's been used in musical lyrics and rhymes for many years. Change your mindset; you were not born to suffer!

A mediocre is a person with a not satisfactory mentality: think about 5 different areas of your life, and honestly assess yourself. Would your score be; very satisfied, satisfied, moderately satisfied, or not satisfied? Anything below very satisfied isn't good enough. There are people, if candidly speaking, will score not satisfied. A not satisfied performance is mediocre performance. Unfortunately, that is where the number is thick.

Except you drive yourself from the position of indolence and average to peak performance, whatever you do can't stand out. Excellence is not achieved by luck; it comes through purpose, plans and actions.

Take a close look at your relationship. Why is it failing? Why aren't you satisfied? What can you do to make it better? Take another close look at your income. Why are you earning that small? How can you improve your earnings? X-ray your entire life, and ask yourself if you're living according to purpose, or just doing what everyone is doing? If you aren't satisfied with your answers, it points to one direction; YOU'VE BEEN LIVING A MEDIOCRE LIFE. Do something about it; change your mindset!

A mediocre is a poor performance mentality: sometimes, a not satisfactory result may not mean poor performance. Some people's performances may be good but not excellent, therefore to them, it is not satisfied. For others, it is a pure expression of being poor. What makes it poorer is because such people have come to accept their circumstances as a norm, so, it becomes a lifestyle. Something that is a lifestyle is difficult to change, especially if the people involved accept it as being okay.

I have an uncle who believes that poverty is the right instrument of humility. He loves being poor because according to him, it keeps him humble. His wrong insinuation is that rich people are arrogant and proud. He's failed to realise that it isn't money that makes you arrogant or proud because, we still have poor people that are.

The poor performance that shouldn't be tolerated in life is the one that affects your purpose in life. If a man does not do well at school or workplace; he must do well in his calling. If he fails in his calling, he is doomed. A poor performance in purpose affects the entirety of a man's vision. Many people are below average in their life's purposes even if some of them earn millions of dollars in other aspects.

A mediocre is a person with inferiority complex mentality: inferiority complex says that you're less important, less valuable and less worthy. It also says that you're low in grade, poor in quality and substandard. Do you want to hear more? Okay, let us go ahead. Inferiority complex says that you're lower in place or position, closer to the bottom or base, and lower in rank, degree or grade. With all these, does it make sense for someone to possess an inferiority complex mentality? No! Inferiority complex mentality is demeaning; mediocre mindset is demeaning.

Who told you that you're less important; who lied to you? Or maybe, you lied to yourself; your mind has been playing funny games on you. Where on earth did you hear that your colour, amount of money in your pocket, academic qualification, nationality, gender, or background must determine how you see yourself? It doesn't matter where you come from, it doesn't matter your sex, it doesn't matter your background, your accent is immaterial; you were born to be a genius, and that is who you truly are. Get out of mediocre mindset; change your mentality; change your mindset!

A mediocre is a person with meagre mentality: meagre is something that is lean, thin or scanty. When you hang around some people, you will be surprise on how lean, thin and scanty they think. Some people don't see the bigger picture because they are myopic in their reasoning. When you go into debate with certain people, their little minds are exposed. For example, racism is a reflection of little minds; corruption is an expression of little minds. There are too many little, lean, thin, and scanty minds around. It doesn't matter who they are, or their high positions; they are still little minds!

Have you noticed meagre minds that base their arguments on ethnicity rather than reasoning? Have you observed some little minds that are dogmatic about religion even if it doesn't make sense? They kill in the name of religion; rape in the name of religion; loot in the name of religion, while others, on the ground of colour, commit unthinkable atrocities; all because of meagre mindsets and their lean, thin and scanty mentalities.

A mediocre is a person with second rate mentality: although some people believe that they're good, but in the corner of their minds, there's always one person that they feel will always be better than them. Because of that belief, no matter how hard they work, that person continues doing better than them. These types of people possess a second rate mentality. For them, if that person isn't in the competition, they believe that they'll be first, but mere sighting the person turns their belief into second position, even if they've prepared so hard.

I am not saying that there may not be anyone whose skills may be better than yours, but stereotyping that belief is detrimental to your progress. If the person is human, he/she is beatable; that's what you should stick into your skull. You may not be able to beat the person; that doesn't mean that you can't beat the person. Circumstances do change; a change of circumstance can make you emerge the winner.

When the prolific Carl Lewis was the Olympics 100 metres champion, he appeared unbeatable, but on the long run, he was beaten.

Change your mindset; step out of mediocrity. Stop that ugly attitude of being second best. You can't win a championship by always being second best. You are number one. Believe it; become it!

A mediocre is a person with indifferent mentality: I hate indifference; I don't mind a negative person but not an indifferent person. Indifference is not average; it is heartlessness and wickedness.

Nothing moves an indifferent person, no matter how much you try. An indifferent person will not argue or debate with you; he will keep silent but still goes ahead to do what is on his mind.

I know someone that is indifferent; his attitude is appalling. When everyone is crying, his face is motionless; when everyone is laughing; his posture remains the same. What he wants to do; he does. What he doesn't want to do, no one can make him do it.

Indifferent people have terrible poor interpersonal skills, and they are not team players. Some of them think their attitude is a reflection of independence but it is insane mediocrity. If nothing moves you, to show emotion for those who hurt, you are a first class mediocre.

Change your mindset; change your attitude!

The Poverty Mindset

No government can eradicate poverty; if it were possible, there wouldn't be any trace of it in the Western World. The reason it is impossible to eradicate poverty is because it is a mindset. If for instance, a nation decides to equally redistribute her income, in a few years, some people will end up being poor. It goes to show that poverty is not a lack of money, but understanding. If it was lack of money, how come some lottery winners end up broke after a few years in spite of the fact that they never lost money in any investment; some of them never even invest. The first thing I hear most lottery winners say, when asked their next line of action is that they want to go on holidays; many hardly think about investments. There are many indications that point to a poverty mindset. Some people may have money but still possess that mentality; there are multimillionaires with poverty mindsets. Yes, they have money, but the deposits of habits that previous poverties have dealt on them linger on. Until they realise it, and deal with it, they may die with it.

There are symptoms evidenced in people with poverty mindsets, and sadly, some people manifest one or more of these symptoms. What are these symptoms?

53

A poverty mindset is devoid of creative ideas: everyday, a wealthy mind generates winning ideas even if he doesn't need them for the moment. A continuous mental generation of meaningful and useful information makes the mind active and purposeful. A wealthy mind thinks through challenges and comes up with strategic solutions, but a poor mind cannot imagine creatively.

A man that is truly poor can rescue himself from the jaws of poverty if he knows how to think. Breakthrough ideas are mostly birthed in the atmosphere of deep thoughts, not worry. Instead of a poor mind, thinking, he worries; worry is the biggest cause of poverty. Some rich men with poverty mindsets have ended up in literal poverties because they spent their money treating the illnesses they incurred from getting worried. A worried mind can never be a creative mind. No good idea comes from the inner recesses of a worried man.

So, the first reflection of poverty mindset is lack of creative ideas. A man with bales of money, but without ideas, is a poor man. Raw cash does not make you rich; it is ideas on how to multiply the cash that does. Why are most countries in Africa poor in spite of the abundance of natural resources? The reason is because, the man with the idea of how to process the raw material is the expert, and like most experts, he makes most of the money. This can also be compared to talent hunt. Most people with talents either don't know they have it, or don't know how to process it. So, the people with the ideas, discover the talents, refine it, and decide how much the talent owner earns. That is why the big Oil industries will continue to be richer than most nations that they tap oil from. No matter how talented and rich a footballer is, he cannot be richer than the one who pays him. The one who pays him has the business idea; so he makes most of the money. Step out of poverty mindset; think with your head; be creative.

A poverty mindset is an ignorant mentality: ideas are different from thorough education. Thorough education offers the laid down principles, the technical methods of doing things, and the direction in which things should go. Please be informed that education is formal and informal; both are very relevant in deciding the destiny of a person, community, and society at large. You may not have gone to school, but if you don't see the need for those after you (your children, for instance) to go, you have a poverty mindset. Losing an opportunity to acquire good education isn't a crime, what is a crime is you letting those around you lose the same privilege because of your ignorance. There are parents or carers who don't care if their children or wards do their home works or not; these people have poverty mindset. There are those who don't bother checking the updates of their children's performances in school; these people have poverty mindset. Ignorance is poverty personified.

Ignorance isn't only expressed in form of lack of education; there are many ignorant educated people everywhere. If you don't understand a thing, but not humble enough to allow those who do teach you, what a poor man you are? Pride is a poor man because he's an inflated balloon, full of ordinary air; with a little poke, he bursts!

A poverty mindset is a mentality lacking in determination and fight: a poverty mindset does not fight; he accepts the status quo. The one with a wealthy mind says to himself, 'I can't die where my fathers did. I must get up and fight until I win'. If your parents couldn't make it, does that mean that you too can't make it? If none of your family members succeeded, does that mean that you too will become a failure? I have never seen a determined man that failed in his pursuits. I have never seen a good fighter surrender until he wins. Anyone who gives up before the battle is won is not just a coward but a poor man. Wealthy minds don't give up; they fight on until they win.

A poverty mindset is a mentality lacking in goals and purpose: the purpose of a footballer on the pitch is to score goals. If you don't know your purpose, you have a poor mind. The purpose of a thing gives it a meaning. With meaning, there is direction. How can a man win if he does not set and score goals? If you put money into the hands of someone without goals and purpose, he won't be able to account for it. Poverty isn't truly lack of money; it is a mindset.

Some people have been handed golden opportunities to succeed in their endeavours; they blew it because they had no purpose and goal.

There was a young lady from a very poor home in a remote area in a country in Africa. In their family, they could hardly feed themselves. One day, a woman travelled from London and saw her wasting away. She had pity on her, and decided to take her to the UK to live with her. In the UK, she was put in school, but unfortunately, this young lady mixed up with the wrong crowd, and started living prodigally. No amount of intervention could help her, as she was determined to toll the road of waywardness. One day, the woman tricked her; she was told that they were all going on holidays to her country. When they arrived, the woman took her passport, and handed her back to her parents.

Because the young lady didn't understand the purpose for which she was taken to England, she blew the opportunity of developing her life, especially in acquiring quality education.

A poverty mindset does not understand the relevance of purpose. A poverty mindset does not realise the power of setting goals. Without goals, success is an illusion. Without purpose, life is without aim and direction. I wish everyone would know and pursue a purposeful and goal specific life!

56

A poverty mindset is a mentality lacking in entrepreneurial skills: one word that scares most people especially those with poverty mindsets is entrepreneurship. They think that owning an enterprise requires the whole world. They fail to understand that by nature, everyone is an entrepreneur.

Who is an entrepreneur? By dictionary definition, an entrepreneur is a person who organises and manages a thing with considerable risk and initiative. Now the question is; have you ever managed and organised something that you thought had an element of risk and required a measure of initiative? If your answer is yes, then you are an entrepreneur! If you are, why not apply the same strategy in starting up a business that you can call yours? A business does not always involve buying and selling, production or manufacturing, etc. Pursuing your purpose in life, using the relevant skills daily, targeted towards profitability, makes you an entrepreneur. Your profit may not, initially be calculated in terms of cash, but one day, as you continue to carry out that assignment that is linked to your passion, it will begin to yield monetary values.

You must do away with that ugly attitude of thinking that you're not cut out for business; it is a poverty mindset borne out of ignorance. Making your talent work is big business; that makes you an entrepreneur.

A poverty mindset is a mentality lacking in prioritisation: prioritisation is the arrangement of tasks, plans, assignments, responsibilities, etc according to their order of importance. A poverty mindset does not understand importance. A father that goes to buy an expensive sports car, while still living in a 2-bed shared apartment with a family of four, definitely does not understand importance. A student that spends ten hours a week partying and one hour studying does not understand importance. An employer that delays the payment of staff salaries and wages in order to make more interests from the bank does not understand importance. A mother that prefers to buy the best makeup at the expense of putting healthy food on the table for her family does not understand importance. I can go on and on.

In prioritisation, first thing must come first; if first thing goes into the middle, it is a reflection of irresponsibility; and irresponsibility is offspring of poverty mindset.

Lack of prioritisation creates unnecessary backlog. If you visit some people's offices, you will find heaps of files that should have been attended to weeks before. If you have access to some people's minds, you will see important goals that were set years ago unachieved - they were busy dealing with issues that were of low relevance while their dream of reaching the sky was slipping away.

If you don't understand the relevance of scale of preference, you have a poverty stricken mindset even if you have the whole money on earth. Remember, a poverty mindset isn't lack of money; it is lack of proper understanding.

A poverty mindset is a mentality lacking in focus: without focus, there is no direction. Focus makes you see one thing, believe in one thing and follow one thing. Focus is the action that makes you concentrate on achieving your purpose in life. Focus is the vision that helps you maintain a positive action until you reach that destination that you behold in your creative imagination.

People with poverty mindsets don't have focus because they want to become everything, do everything, but end up becoming and doing nothing. Rather than pick and begin with a niche, a poverty mindset picks the whole marketplace, when it is obvious that he can't reach more than 1% of the market. Rather than begin from small, a poverty mindset begins from big, and ends up very small.

A man without focus doesn't know what he wants. If he doesn't know, he copies everything that appears good and flashy. Another man's dream appears attractive to a person with poverty mindset; that is the major problem. If a person can't see his own destination and dreams, he slips into nightmare. Nightmare looks like a dream, but it is horrific. Nightmare casts a man into pandemonium. He thinks he's seeing and heading somewhere, but where he goes is a threat to his destiny.

Until you sort out your reason for existence, what you call a dream is nightmare. A focus on nightmare is inconceivable deception because it takes you far away from the right direction. There are many young people seeing nightmares but conclude that they're dreaming. They think one day, they will wake up in paradise, but the hell of life awaits them.

Drug addiction is nightmare; wake up from your sleep and be real to yourself; you've lost it. Crime is nightmare; you seem to be the only one in your own world hoodwinking yourself. Second by second, time is running out; day by day, the night is falling. Soon, you'll look back and ask yourself what you did with your life. Get out of where you are; change your mindset. No one can do it for you; you have to do it yourself. The onus is on you; it's daybreak folk. Wake up! Wake up!! Wake up!!!

A poverty mindset is mentality of wastefulness and extravagance: many people buy what they don't need simply because it is either cheap or a promotional offer. Sometimes, it may not be cheap or on promotion but just appealing to the eyes. A lot of money has been flushed down the toilet system buying things that shouldn't be bought. I used to be in the same boat until I went through one of the toughest financial moments of my life. While in that situation, with a wife and two children, I became homeless. Then, when I see $1, it will appear like $1M. Before then, I would go to shops and buy things I may never use or don't need, but while in the mess, I began to learn how to be thrifty is money management. Now, if I don't need it, I don't buy it. Even if I need it, I will take a closer look if the value equates the amount; if it doesn't, I will shop around until I see the one that has value for money. Never again, will I go through that darkness! Never, never, never again!!

Waste and extravagance are quickest ways to poverty. If you are wasteful, you're inadvertently inviting the day of lack; the day of lack is the day of nothing; the day of lack is the day of poverty. When you waste that food, the bellies of the hungry children all over the world will call for your judgment. When you buy that clothes that you don't need, the frozen skins of naked people that can't afford the cheapest clothes will cry out against you. Don't be wasteful; don't be extravagant.

Days before writing this chapter of the book, I read online, the interview granted by an African multimillionaire king. He was bragging about his expensive Rolls Royce, $1M wrist watch, fleet of cars, and affluence. He was berated by a lot of people that read the piece because, in his own kingdom are many people that don't know where they can find the day's meal, yet, a so called leader of a people would insensitively appear on a magazine to boast of his self centredness. In my conclusion, he is a poor man. That is the way poor people think and talk!

A poverty mindset is pilferage mentality: when I left the University, I was jobless, and so, I made a friend in my community that almost led me astray. He was the son of a millionaire, who has lost his way. One day, while standing in front of a health and beauty store, we saw that the shop assistant was fast asleep. My friend took advantage of the situation and entered into the shop. He took a facial cream and hid it inside his pocket. I thought he was playing pranks, but he actually stole it. That was the day I began reconsidering my relationship with him. When I parted with him, he continued with his pilfering behaviour. The sad thing is that his attitude later pushed him into early grave; he's late.

What would the son of a millionaire do with stealing a facial cream? It doesn't make sense; I don't know if it does to you. If he wanted a shop of that cream, he could afford it, so, why does he have to steal it? Poverty mindset will make a person steal what he can afford.

Another form of pilferage is adultery. Yes; adultery! It is equivalent to stealing what does not belong to you. Adultery isn't modernisation; even if today's world is beginning to shut their eyes on it; it is pilfering. Why steal sex, when you can legally have it? It is a poverty mindset that does such things! Pilfering money that doesn't belong to you is poverty mindset. Whether as an employee or employer, you have a poor mind, if you pilfer each others money.

Until I found an answer to it, anytime I shaved, I usually had bumps. A friend helped by referring me to a shop to buy a certain type of clipper. After making the purchase, I asked the shop owner if he had any good aftershave. He brought out an alum stone and did what every good marketer would do; promote the relevance of the product. He offered to sell it 50% cheaper than its actual price because it was a bit broken, and I was full of appreciation; I started referring people to the shop. One day, on a second thought, I decided to walk into the next shop after his, and was flabbergasted when I observed that I was cheated by over 150% increase of what the man sold on promotion. That was my last day in that shop!

Pilferage, in whatever form it comes, makes you a loser. Deliberately overcharging people to make over-profit is stealing.

61

If you don't know the competitive price, it makes a whole lot of sense as a business person to find out; such dubious ignorance is not an excuse.

A poverty mindset is an emotional-spender mentality: what do I mean by emotional spending? As an African, I will speak from African perspective. In my community, there are strong family ties; your cousin is your brother or sister; your neighbour is considered your aunty or uncle if he's older. There is this emotional attachment among the African setting, and this makes us live more in unity. Like every other culture, this knit also has its pitfalls.

There is a sense of responsibilities among a family setting in African culture. For example, it is your responsibility to take care of your aged parents; it is also partly your responsibility to help send your younger ones to school if you're financially okay.

Many a times, this strong family ties are subject to abuse, for example, I will tell you the story of a one time African student in Canada. This man was struggling to pay the tuition fee of his doctoral programme abroad, and at the same time, doing his best to help his extended family members back home.

One day, he received a phone call from one of his sisters saying that their mother was seriously sick, and that a certain amount of money was needed for her treatment. Out of emotional feelings, without verification, he squeezed the money out, but to later find out that no mother was sick. The most painful part of the story was that the money was used to organise a party.

Emotional spending does not verify before giving away money. The ability to discern before you spend is a golden attribute. The ability to probe before you conclude is a leadership treasure.

Some years ago, someone asked me to give her money for a certain project. I wanted to, but decided that I must probe further before consenting. I said to her, 'tell me the truth. If you're truthful to me, you will get more than you want, but the moment you start deceiving me, when I find out, it will sever the relationship between both of us. What do you actually want the money for?' She opened up and told me the real thing!

Emotional spending is a reflection of poverty mindset. The reason it is, is because most compassionate people that went through poverty don't like others to experience the same thing. As a result, anyone that comes in pretence to be in need is always helped. Due to this, people take advantage of them. There is the need to grow out of that mentality; at least, ask questions before you put your hand into your pocket.

Speaking again from the African perspective, this same issue repeats itself in situations where a person either has only one child or son. There is the tendency of a parent to emotionally spend money on the child independent of whether it is a need or not. On certain occasions, some of these parents have spoilt their children to the extent that they can't be independent. Where a grown up child keeps running back home for financial help, there is a serious parental negligence or irresponsibility.

A poverty mindset is an over-negotiation mentality: I love to negotiate; I teach people to do the same, but what I don't like is not knowing, where to draw the boundary lines. Some people are not negotiating; their intention is to cheat you. That is a poverty mindset.

Negotiation should be a win-win situation; if yours is win-lose situation, you're a cheat, and probably, a thief.

Unconsciously, some people over-negotiate. They always want to win everything while their opponent loses every-thing. The truth is that you can't win everything. If you don't lose sometimes, you won't have the ability to manage failure.

If you can't manage failure, you can't be a good leader. Negotiate, but don't take it beyond the boundary of sanity.

Illiteracy Mindset

Illiteracy is often used to describe people that are uneducated, but what a lot of people haven't realised is that it goes beyond not acquiring secular education; it is a mindset. Many times, we've met people with degrees or other forms of higher qualifications whose attitudes have negatively mesmerised our thoughts, all because they acted in manners that did not portray education. Sometimes, these manners have become habits, so, no one can make excuses for them.

The major definition of illiteracy is the inability to read and write. As the definition goes, the conclusion of most people is that reading and writing only involves the physical identification and interpretation of symbols. But, what most people don't realise is that situations, circumstances, dispositions, and many more unprintable insinuations and environments require reading and writing. Therefore, some people may be highly educated but can't read the handwriting on the wall. Some Chairmen of big corporations are educated but can't read a change in business climate. Some parents are educated but can't read the variation in their children's behaviours. Some spouses are educated but can't read when the relationship slipped into the mud. Illiteracy of the mind is the worst illiteracy in life, but unfortunately, that's where a lot of people have found themselves. Can you see that you may read and write, or even become a top educational researcher, but still have illiteracy mindset?

Apart from the inability to read and write, illiteracy is further defined as the violation of accepted standards in reading and writing. This in essence means that for the fact you're able to read and write does not mean that you're literate. Every reading and writing has its standards; if you don't follow the standard, you aren't literate. Some people can pronounce a word, but wrongly. I do remember that sometime ago, I use to pronounce façade as fa-k-ade. I can read and write, but I didn't follow the standards of the pronunciation. In the same vein, many people think they can read situations but actually misread it because they never followed the standards. Some employees have misread the circumstances in their workplaces, and then put in letters of resignations from jobs that would have led them to their purposes in life. Let us talk a bit about writing because we've been hammering on reading.

There was one woman that thought she was educated; in the literal sense, she was a good writer; she could write volumes of letters, but most of her letters always caused troubles, even to her and her children. When there are issues that require wisdom to tackle, she wouldn't think with her brain before picking up pen and paper to write things that will inflame the situation. She never followed the standard of ethical and common sense writing; in spite of the fact that she thinks she's literate. In her certificate, she's literate, but in her mindset, she's a complete illiterate person.

An illiterate mindset is an uncultured mindset that does not demonstrate common sense knowledge. Where there isn't common sense knowledge, trouble becomes imminent.

Apart from the issues mentioned above, there are many ways people exhibit illiteracy mindset. I have enumerated some of them below.

Illiteracy mindset exhibits rash communication: you need to see the way some people, without caution speak to subordinates, elderly people, mates, or anyone. The flippancy of certain people are sometimes, almost unpardonable.

Every good communication must have respect, caution, subtlety and persuasion embedded in it, but despite some people's postgraduate degrees in communications, they are devoid of the main elements of communications. Education without proper communication furthers ignorance.

When Justine Sacco; the fired PR Director of InterActive Corp (IAC) tweeted, 'Going to Africa. Hope I don't get Aids. Just kidding. I'm white!' that was acute foolishness lacking in common sense. You see, you can speak a professional language but still be stupid if you don't understand common sense language. Some professionals have been flushed through the toilet system because of lack of common sense. Some businesses have folded up because the businessmen or women didn't know common sense; they could strike deals but don't respect deals. Common sense language is vital in maintaining a wholesome wellbeing; without it, the best intelligence cannot help you. Rash communication is a total reflection of lack of common sense, and unfortunately, it is also a reflection of illiteracy mindset.

Illiteracy mindset exhibits lack of etiquette: etiquette is conventional requirements as to social behaviour, proprieties of conduct as established in any class or community or for any occasion. It is also the code of ethical behaviour regarding professional practice or action among the members of a profession in their dealings with each other.

There was someone who contested for a very top job in the world; a household name in certain quarters. One of the reasons he lost was because he most often, wears sandals to conferences, even when he's delivering keynote speeches. For someone about to occupy one of the topmost jobs in the world, that is unethical. People need to realise that the way and manner a person dresses speaks a lot about the person's mindset. Some people say, 'it doesn't matter how I dress; I don't care. It's my life. I'm not here to impress anybody' Really? Realise that life is not all about you; it is collective. If it is collective, you are only a microcosm of the entire population.

If you're a microcosm, decisions aren't onlymade by you. If you think it should be all about you, your self centredness will rob you of good relationships and opportunities.

Etiquette is a conventional requirement; no one is asking you to do anything extraordinary. In medicine, there is a conventional requirement of fashion and procedure before a doctor goes into the theatre to conduct a surgical operation. In the legal system, there is a conventional requirement of fashion and court procedures laid down for lawyers to follow. In conflict management, business, relationship, family, education, and so on, there are conventional requirements to follow. The licenses of some professionals have been withdrawn because they broke the rules of conventional requirements. The contracts of some business people have been terminated because they never adhered to the rules of conventional requirements. Some homes are in tatters because conventional requirements were not followed. Refusal to follow conventional requirements is exhibition of illiteracy mindset. You may have gone to school, but the school hasn't gone through you.

Illiteracy mindset is an always defensive mentality: an attitude that always makes excuses for inefficiencies and inabilities is a defensive attitude. People with defensive attitudes hardly admit their wrongs; they either give multiple emotional and convincing reasons why they were wrong or blame it on other people. Even when they admit, they use languages like, 'I know I am wrong, but....' the 'buts' in their admissions cancel out their admissions. It is difficult to bend defensive people because they're difficult to correct. To understand better the mentality of defensive people, read the scenario below.

Ken: *You should have mopped the milk you spilled on the floor.*

Mr. Defensive: *I'm I the first person that will spill milk on earth.*

Ken: *I know you aren't, but that doesn't stop you from cleaning the mess.*

Mr. Defensive: *Are you calling me a mess?*

Ken: *I didn't call you a mess, all I said was that it makes common sense to clean a mess you made on the floor.*

Mr. Defensive: *So you mean I don't have common sense.*

From the scenario above, it is clear that Mr. Defensive is simply a trouble maker. Which is easier; the long unnecessary argument put up by Mr. Defensive or simply going ahead to clean the mess he made? In true life scenario, some people are like Mr. D; instead of avoiding unnecessary debates or arguments, they elongate what shouldn't be, in order to feed their ego.

An unnecessary defensive mentality is manifestation of illiteracy mindset. Those with mental education are civil in attitude and approach; those whose education only ended in certificates act like they're from the gutters. Degrees and different forms of certificates don't mean you're educated; if education hasn't reached your mind, it hasn't reached your life.

There are different ways people exhibit defensive attitudes; I have only given a scenario.

Some people defend it, when they hurt other people. Rather than say they're sorry, you'll hear words like, 'I didn't do it deliberately'. Do you only apologise when you hurt people deliberately? Does it mean that if you accidently step on someone, you'll walk away without saying sorry because you didn't do it deliberately? Change your mindset; change that mindset.

Illiteracy mindset is an argumentative mentality: argumentative mentality is a bit different from a defensive mindset. In argumentative mentality, the person always wants to win an argument whether he's right or wrong.

While in secondary school, I had a close friend. One day, in another friend's house, we were learning a song. The song had a word, 'hurt', but my friend preferred calling it 'hunt'. I pointed it to him that it was 'hurt' and not 'hunt', but in spite of glaring evidences, he argued from day until evening, and for years before we lost touch, he wouldn't accept that he was wrong.

To an argumentative person, the satisfaction of winning an argument is better than the benefit of gaining knowledge. What is the essence of acquiring certificates when it cannot be used for the transformation of the mind?

Argumentative mentality is offspring of illiteracy mindset. I haven't said that one cannot be involved in a debate or argue out a point or defend your beliefs; what I have said is that if truth is glaring, and you're truly convinced that it is, why not humbly admit it? We know you're more intelligent than the person that birth the truth, but mental intelligence accepts established truths rather than isomerise it in order to stamp your name on it. Grow up; change that mindset!

Illiteracy mindset is a non-teachable spirit: a non-teachable spirit is different from people with learning difficulties. There are people that find it difficult to understand when taught, and there are also others that it takes a longer time to comprehend. In one of my articles published on my blog, I have recommended 'repetition' as answer to people with low level of comprehension.

A person with non-teachable spirit may not be an argumentative person, but a person that is unwilling to learn new things; a person that isn't flexible. New technologies are coming up daily, and these technologies are beginning to win over different professions and disciplines. Software are now available for doing different things. For example, there are lots of accounting software. For an accountant that is accustomed to using only calculators, things have changed. If the accountant does not change with time, he will lose his clienteles.

In spite of change, some people are unwilling to change. They keep making excuses with age, yet, there are older people that have seen the light, embraced change, and started excelling in the new direction. Such people have fused the old and the new, and are making huge profits because they come with experience plus innovation, and that makes them more relevant.

Without adopting purposeful change, you'll lose your relevance. History alone cannot save you from a fall, if you're not willing to embrace the present and the future. Some people die untimely deaths with their experiences because they have refused to accept the reality of today. Don't get me wrong; some ancients are unchangeable, but technology, creativity and innovation do not fall into that category.

Illiteracy mindset repeatedly falls into the same error: do many people ever learn from their errors; do they ever learn from their mistakes? Some do, but the fact on ground is that many people don't.

Some people have divorced twice or thrice, based on the same error. Some people have failed examinations twice or thrice, making the same mistake. Sometimes you wonder if they ever learnt anything from the errors of the past.

Illiteracy mindset falls into the same error repeatedly, consciously or unconsciously. Some people get out of a relationship, and without further ado, jump into another, without taking some time to evaluate the previous one.

Without evaluation, you can't estimate the causal effects and how to deal with, or avoid the mistakes that were made.

You claim to have gone to school, but how come, you repeated the same mistake that got you fired in your previous job? I know you have a doctoral degree in Mathematics, but how come, your son failed the subject in his Ordinary Level examination? You definitely did not play your role! Leadership makes mistakes but corrects them. If you keep falling into the same error, you're ignorant. Ignorance is illiteracy. If it is repeated ignorance; it has become a habit; if it is a habit; it has slipped into a mindset. Wake up from your slumber; change that mindset!

Illiteracy mindset eschews personal development: like the word goes, 'personal'. It means a development that comes out of your own conviction; not the one you're forced to do. A development that emanates from personal conviction indicates that you're a self motivated person. Shame; some people aren't?

If your education stopped where your parents took you to, you are not a self motivated person. If your training ended where your employers took you to; you are not a self motivated person. Self motivated people don't wait to be pushed before taking purposeful developmental actions.

To broaden your mind, you must keep developing your mind. To earn higher than your mates, you must keep developing yourself. To occupy better positions in life, you must keep developing yourself. Spend money on your brain; not on your hair. I am not saying that you shouldn't maintain your hair, but if your hair is finer than your brain, you are a problem to humanity. There are lots of people on the benefit system with beautiful hairs but burden to the society. Be an asset, not a burden. What will make you an asset is your undying drive for personal development.

Illiteracy mindset endeavours to stop other people's growth and development: if you work with a boss from hell, even if you don't go to hell, you'll smell hell. Smelling hell is terrible because it stinks worse than rotten eggs and beans combined.

Some bosses are crazy! They stop people's promotions; they stop their organisations from training staffs under them by making senseless recommendations, all because of their sadistic behaviours. Some people enjoy seeing subordinates in pains; they derive pleasure from it. If you have such an attitude, I've got five words for you; YOU HAVE AN ILLITERACY MINDSET.

You can't go up, when you don't create space for people under you to go up. No wonder you've also remained on the same position. Yes, I mean, on the same position in spite of the fact that you were given a promotion. Your employer may promote you, while life demotes you. You may have so much money in your bank account while you, at the same time, have so much trouble in your life account. Life brings back to you, a million fold of what you give to others. Sadism to people yields extra sadism to self. If you make people go up, you'll go up; if you pull them down, you're definitely going down.

Permit people's development; be interested in people's growth. What does it cost you? Nothing! What do you profit from enhancing the life of humanity? Everything! Stop killing growth; stop murdering development. Be mentally educated; change that mindset!

Illiteracy mindset enjoys having lots of titles: title mentality is common among black people, especially Africans. Thank God, I am a black African, so no one will accuse me of racism. Have you ever taken a look at some people's titles? You will see things like; Professor. Kenneth Nkemnacho B.Sc, M.Sc, PhD, DSC, FCA.

72

What a heck? Give me a break! I don't think that there's any need for all that. Simply pick the highest title and forget the preceding ones; that makes a whole lot of sense. Displaying all your profiles, when it isn't curriculum vitae, to me, is exhibition of illiteracy mindset. Life isn't all about titles but your ability to purposefully apply what you've learnt into making life better for humanity. Steve Jobs didn't have all that profile, but created something that is prolific; Apple. Bill Gate didn't have all that profile, but came up with Microsoft. The world is looking for values, not titles.

I remember the story that one of my lecturers in the University told us. He was then, a senior lecturer but not a professor. Though not a professor, his achievements in the area of biochemical researches were globally recognised. He said, anytime they went on scientific conferences, after being dazzled by some junior scientists, most professors from my country will warn them not to use the title, 'professor' for them, because in spite of their titles, there's nothing tangible to show for it.

In professional circles also, there have been craze for titles. Having lived in the western world for years, I have never seen an engineer use titles like, 'I am Engineer Kenneth' it is usually Mr. I have never also, seen an account say, 'I am Chartered or Qualified Account Kenneth' they simply use Mr. or whatever, as the case may be. Or simply, they just use their names without titles. But in certain countries or ethnicities, in order to feel more important than others, irrelevant and unconventional titles are attached to names. It does not make sense! Using it, does not mean you're good at what you do. It is your diligence that will make you stand out, not your titles. A title mentality is illiteracy mentality!

The Ethnic Mindset

All over the world, the main element of division is ethnicity. From the Tower of Babel to Tower Hamlet, ethnicity has caused more problems for humanity. No matter how much, different governments preach the doctrine of social integration, in the mind of man, where he comes from, and his anthropological association play major roles in his behaviour and disposition to life.

To make it more serious, within certain ethnic groups are fragmented micro-ethnicities, thereby making tolerance for one another very difficult to attain. The ethnic mindset is the most dangerous mindset.

Recently in India, a couple of weeks before writing this chapter, something happened. A 20 year old woman from Birbhum District in West Bengal was gang-raped by 13 men on the orders of a village court as punishment for having a relationship with a man from a different community. One would have thought that in this age of civilisation, such things shouldn't be heard of, let alone, happening. But the human mind is such that, if not properly informed, it cannot be transformed. The information does not necessarily come from secular education because schools don't teach change of mindsets; the information for transformation comes from the willingness to embark on purposeful personal development.

Most of the wars around the world, especially civil wars are emergent of ethnic mindset. The Bosnian war was as a result of ethnic mindset. Due to this, thousands of lives were lost. The Rwandan and Sierra Leonean wars were due to ethnic mindsets; one ethnic group believed they were better than the other, and therefore embarked on ethnic cleansing.

The ethnic mindset does not only occur in third world or developing nations; in the most advanced worlds, it is very prominent as we will see later in this chapter. In the streets of New York, London, Paris, Berlin, Sydney, and many more, ethnic mindset is ripping the world apart because man has found it difficult to condone and respect another man's originality. The mentality of ethnic superiority is damaging the world and eluding it of most needed peace.

Hitler is gone, but many Hitlers have been born. These Hitlers may not go into literal warfare, but the psychological wars that go on daily in our world cannot be documented. So, in pretence, we live in false peace until the bubble bursts. Xenophobic violence is the aftermath of ethnic mindset. Asking people to go home, a slogan commonly used by indigenes against migrants, is due to ethnic mindset. Unfortunately, some government policy makers are beginning to mimic the voice of ethnicity, which in turn makes hypocritical, their call for multicultural integration.

The United States Senator, Marco Rubio says, 'We are special because we've been united not by a common race or ethnicity. We're bound together by common values. That family is the most important in society. That Almighty God is the source of all we have.' Again, Ana Monnar, an American teacher of Cuban origin writes, 'Choose your friends and mates, not by the money in their bank account, creed, ethnicity, or color; instead, choose character, actions, heart, and soul. When we bleed, we bleed the same color.'

I wish everyone will see like the two people above, then, our thinking will be well shaped to deal with the internal storms brewed by our perceived divergence. We can't win the world by hating other people's worlds. No debate is won by hacking off, the heads of opponents. Genuine love is what conquers; hate is always conquered. To be on the winning side, you must be on the love side. Anything that contradicts pure love makes you a lifetime loser. As long as the world remains, there will continue to be different ethnic groups. The earlier you change your mindset, the better for you. Change that mindset!

The Various Types of Ethnic Mindset

The racial mindset: race is the classification of humans based on skin colour, facial forms, or eye shape, and of recent, genetic markers such as blood group; the most predominant being skin colour.

For hundreds of years, if not thousands, skin colour has been a major factor of discrimination. It is unimaginable that a man would like a shoe colour but when he sees it on human, instantly, he hates it. Many people like black shoes, but one wonders why any sane human being that loves wearing black shoes and suits will hate a black person. That is absolute insanity. To make the situation worse, some so called experts, politicians and social scientists have equated black skin to lack of intelligence. How wrong they are!

It may suffice you to know that racism isn't just against black people; some blacks hate whites, and they rationalise it by citing the innumerable incidences of whites hating blacks, but that isn't enough excuse to hate another man's colour. Muhammad Ali says, 'Hating people because of their color is wrong. And it doesn't matter which color does the hating. It's just plain wrong.'

There are many cases of racism across the world. One area it has been so noticeable is in sports, especially football. The ridiculous thing is that some fans do racist chants against black players in their own teams.

On 24 November 2013, there was a La Liga football match between Sevilla and Real Betis. Real Betis player, Paulao was sent off for two yellow card offences, and to his utmost surprise, sections of the Real Betis supporters started making monkey chants and obscene gestures towards him; a black Brazilian player. That was shocking! Even if it shouldn't be tolerated, it is understandable when the opposing team's supporters act in such unacceptable manner, but for your team supporters to do so, is unbelievable. This is the level that racial mindset has taken the world.

Racism is a form of ethnic mindset. This mindset assumes that a specific colour is better than the other or others. In the mindset of a racist, he develops an artistic philosophy that is shambolic and off course. Unfortunately, secular education cannot address the problem of racism because there are professors and professionals that are specialists in imposing the doctrine of racism. In many researches conducted by some white European and American social scientists, with bias, they conclude that black colours are never-do-well; white colours are superior to any other race. Because they have the voice and media, these conclusions play their dramas in the minds of their hearers. As a result, the weak white mind imbibes their conclusions and acts on it, thereby creating more social problems. The weak black mind, who believes that he's a never-do-well, resorts to crime, and ends up never doing well. When this happens, the same experts come out to reiterate that in the first place, they were right. But their expectation from the onset was to play on the minds of their hearers in order to stir them up for negativity. When you understand, and never bring their expectations to fruition, they are shocked, and then look for other media of frustrating an un-liked colour.

Racism is a game designed by those whose intention is to oppress, but too sad to say, those who play the game don't understand the motive behind it, because the designers make it, and then step aside to analyse the statistics. Don't be a victim of evil statistics. The best way the world can move forward for good is through healthy relationships independent of the colour of the skin or eyes. Without pure conscience towards one

77

another, the colour of the skin is immaterial. Dignity isn't borne out of race; it is borne out of the character to love one another, respect one another, and believe in each others destinies in spite of origin.

There is a whole new dimension to racism; people hating their own colours. Self-colour hate makes people inflict injuries upon themselves. In winter, skin colour is lighter but in summer, it glows because of skin fats being melted by the heat, so, there's what is called high fluidity of the cell membrane. Each change of colour per season, serves its own purpose in the interest of man, but the sad thing is that certain man prefers a specific type, and so, pushes it beyond measure, and as a result, it backfires. I've got nothing against tanning the skin, but how come, certain people tan until the skin becomes cancerous? It doesn't make sense to me.

Let us address the issue of skin bleaching among certain black people. Apart from the health consequence, a bleached skin is ugly to behold. It's time people realise that beauty isn't measured by the colour of the skin. A light complexion doesn't make you a beauty queen or a handsome man. Skin bleaching is a racial mindset that has degenerated into inferiority complex. If you hate your skin colour, in my opinion, you are a racist, and you have a psychological problem.

The Religious Mindset: let me make it abundantly clear that no man can fight for God. If He created the whole universe, it means that He's more than powerful to fight for Himself.

The number one problem of religious mindset is ignorance and lack of common sense. Why a man will not sit down to ponder on the possibility of the knowledge he's been fed before acting on it, is a big question I still cannot answer. Should a man blow himself up to make a point? I don't think it is the right thing to do. Should a man murder other people for the sole reason of imposing his beliefs? That shouldn't ever happen, if only man can think before he acts.

One unfortunate thing that happens is that most of the people being murdered share a common belief, not in terms of suicidal and murderous ideologies, but in terms of belonging to the same faith. If your intention is to make people of other beliefs imbibe yours, why kill those that are already on your side? You see, a religious mindset makes no common sense and has no common sense. As some misguided Muslims kill fellow Muslims, they also have zero tolerance for people of other religions.

In all faiths, you have those that have chosen to be fundamentalists. Recently, in Bangui, Central African Republic, some so called Christians have taken up arms against Muslim neighbours; killing and maiming them. As a Christian, I'm wondering what portion of the Bible they can cite to support their actions. They may have read, turn the other cheek, as, slap the other person's cheek. Or, maybe, they read; love your neighbour as yourself, as, love yourself more than your neighbour. In religion, man devices his own ideology in order to satisfy his selfish endeavours. As he does this, he wins souls to himself because weak minds are willing to follow anyone who wakes up one morning to say that he is God. Because religion is blind, those who follow, hardly ask purposeful soul searching questions. They just follow like fools, until they get to the point of no return!

There is another subtle religion that is gradually emerging. It is called the worship of man! This religion cuts across all major religions. In the worship of man, the one that is being worshiped plays on the mentality of the people. He makes them believe that he has the most access to Divinity; he is the main person that is closer to God. So, everyone, rather than take their pleas to God, depend on him to do it. With this, he draws attention to himself. It is good business for a person that has the attention of many people. So, he milks them, and dries them up, until they're dead. In spite of the dryness and deadness, some people keep believing in the cheats because in the mindset of man, he believes in his incapability. When he sees a man that says he's capable, he relies on that man to reach the unseen on his behalf. This sect of religion is selling so much in our dispensation. People must realise that divine relationship is personal. Though we need mentors, don't make a mentor a God.

Religion makes it hard for people to maximise their innate potentials. It blocks the true essence of man from actualising his purpose. Religion is a killer. If it isn't, why do certain religions prevent a dying man from taking blood transfusion, if that is the only way to make him live? Why do some, completely stop their members from taking medications?

God isn't religious. If He was, He wouldn't give man the power of choice. God gives you the power of choice, and then holds you accountable for your decisions. Religion gives no choice; it forces you to do what you don't want to do, and then holds you accountable for her decision.

The Class Mindset: the class mindset I am addressing is a group of persons sharing similar social position and certain economic, political, and cultural characteristics. There's nothing wrong with belonging to a class, especially a top one, as it gives you the privilege to network with great people, which may inherently, impact positively on your vision and purpose in life. What I don't find convenient is having a class mindset. What is a class mindset? A class mindset is one that looks down or demeans those below, or worships those above. Those who look down on other people because of their lower positions in social status don't have the quality of empathy, and they end up descending in a shameful way. Muammar Al-Gaddafi, unfortunately, made this statement, 'I am an international leader, the dean of the Arab rulers, the king of kings of Africa and the imam of Muslims, and my international status does not allow me to descend to a lower level.' No one is asking anyone above to descend, but from the top, have a feeling for those below. Any genuine feeling for those below will make every effort to pull them up. It is understandable that no matter how much you try to pull some people up, they prefer staying down, because they don't have the character to stay up, but in spite of that, do the best you can to take people up. That is true leadership!

Those who worship people because of their top positions in society don't have the confidence to pursue their own dreams and become better in life. We should celebrate people, but we shouldn't worship. Worshipers do crazy things. Some, in a bid to be like their idols, change their identities to look like those they worship. Some people worship Michael Jackson, they want to look like him in every ramification, and so, this makes them lose their own identities. A man with a stolen identity is fraudulent. He may not have stolen a credit card, but he has lost his credit to someone else. A man who loses his credit to someone else loses his dream. If he loses his dream, he loses his future. If he loses his future, he loses his destiny. Without knowing your destination, even when you're given a roadmap, its essence becomes useless.

Class consciousness is negative-pride consciousness. Class consciousness deliberately imposes the mentality of a ghetto in a society in order to create compartmentalisation. When compartments are created, those that think they're better than others, build fences around their boundaries in order to ward off those they consider to be mortals.

When I first relocated to United Kingdom, there was this cliché, even believed and accepted by those it concerned, that Hackney is the poorest Borough in London. Then, I would look at the environment, and compare it with other boroughs, but in my lay man's assessment, I couldn't see any major visible difference. My conclusion was that the forces at work, somehow, want to play on the mindset of this community, so as to introduce pictures of inferiority. As it has always been, where a mental picture of dark ages is painted, the people keep having nightmares. With nightmares, you're heading nowhere.

Those with class mindset will do everything possible to maintain their statuses. They hack the minds of potential competitors, and introduce viruses that they will spend their whole lifetime curing. The need to be well prevents those they make sick from fighting for potential laurels. So, they bow. They may keep bowing till they die; except they find a quick cure; they may bow into their graves with dreams unaccomplished.

The Culture Mindset: I have previously talked about culture while introducing the mindset, but I think there is the need to focus on the youth and consumer culture.

There isn't doubt about the relevance of youth to every society. That is why the youth mindset needs thorough attention. The youth culture mustn't be a binge drinking culture, but unfortunately, that is what some people have deemed it to be. The youth culture shouldn't be a crime culture, but it is almost appearing to be. Gangsterism has been painted in a very attractive way, so as to attract young people with weak minds, and a lot are heading into it. Why a young person thinks shooting or stabbing another person makes him or her superstar is what doesn't make sense to a rational being. Our jails are filled with young people, and even now, our mental health institutions have a high record of youth because it takes an additional substance to act in some unbelievable violent ways. Drug addiction is soaring among young people while most parents watch helplessly and hopelessly. Yes, some governments are doing the best they can to tackle this evil, while some, look on as if it doesn't concern them. In spite of some concerted efforts, the decadence escalates because providing social amenities alone isn't enough to deal with what goes on in the head of humanity. Except you tackle his inside, anything outside provides little or no solution. What is needed, to deal with this rising crisis are mindset-focused programmes, but unfortunately, many governments have taken spiritual and mental developmental programmes out of school curriculums. Not only have they done that, they have also made them appear like evil in the sight of our young people. So, with their hands, they have created problems, and then spend taxpayers' money to seek solutions where they can't be found. This solution seeking adventure creates additional portfolios for politicians, who day and night act like they have the answers to all problems.

What the youth need is a change of mindset. What controls the actions of a man, are the thoughts and pictures in his heart. If you make him think right and see right, he will act right. Our prison yards will be empty if our mindsets change. The police will have no need to arrest anyone, if our mindsets change. Someone may say that sanity will make some people jobless, but my answer is no. If we think right and act right, we will become more innovative; innovation creates more purposeful jobs.

The consumer culture is a spender culture. A spender only buys; he doesn't create anything. As a black person, I want to be a bit critical in challenging my community; we need to do more in areas of creativity. Music and sports are great, but someone made the guitars, pianos, footballs, or racing cars. If they hadn't, our talents will be hidden. We buy too much but create little. I'm tired of all the excuses we make about slavery, colonialism, racism and other forms of discrimination. What we should realise is that great innovations are born out of adversities, not comfort. Deprivation should challenge us to look for other means of doing things, rather than depressing us. If we see discrimination as a call for purposeful action, we will wake up and think. In any positive thought is a positive

83

mental picture. Pictures are the first step to creativity. Let us stop buying things we can make; let us go ahead and make them.

While working as a market researcher, during lunch breaks, I was always at Gregg's buying sandwiches and drinks, but my white colleagues would make their sandwiches from home and come with drinks which were a lot cheaper. One day, I asked myself what it will cost me to make ordinary sandwiches if it isn't because of my consumer mindset. I changed that mindset.

Most of the products imported by Africa, they already have the raw materials, but the skills to process them are the major challenges. It shouldn't have been a challenge if good policies that target creativity are implemented. Our educational policies are skewed; you have Computer Science graduates that can't operate the computer or Engineers that can't design a simple programme. All we do is memorise content of dated textbooks. That is why we rely on the western world for handouts; I mean foreign aids because we haven't got the skills to aid ourselves.

Rather than wait for the government, I encourage everyone to take his destiny into his hand by endeavouring to be creative. Let us turn down the mentality of consumer culture; let us embrace creativity. That is the only way the world will respect us. That is the only way the world will stop dictating for us. That is true independence!

CHAPTER FOUR

WHAT YOU SHOULD DO TO BE RESOLUTE

Every icon I have followed or studied; past or present, have something in common; resoluteness. Each and every one of them resolved in his heart and action to surpass the boundary lines of obstacles, and their resolutions made them have great results. Those that beat cancer beat them by resolution. Those that overcame poverty, first resolved in their hearts to fight that devil that always makes your pocket empty, and they won. Nothing outstanding can be achieved without a made-up mind. If your mind is made-up to reach your goal and hit your target, no lion or bear can stop you.

People with resolute minds don't depend on luck. They know that on the tallest mountains are the best things in life, so, they're ready to climb until they reach the top to take what they want. As they climb, midway, like every other person, they get discouraged, feel tired, and become despondent, but their hunger for excellence keeps them going. As a result, they are self motivated. Most often, they need no one to fire them up; they already have their fires within. Daily, they kindle that fire, to warm themselves up as they push their ways towards the actualisation of that vision. The fire they kindle also becomes illumination for them in the nights of their pursuits. To be honest, every vision has a night time!

If you want to be an icon, be resolute. The road to success is full of mountains; if it were easy, everyone would be there, but it isn't, so, you need to imbibe the culture of a made-up mind. When your mind is made up, no bully on your way is big enough to send you back home. Every icon burnt his comfort zone before setting out on the journey. If you still have somewhere to run back to, you haven't decided what you want yet. If you have no home behind you, you will not look back. If your comfort is ahead of you, you will forge forward, no matter how far it is. Don't be weary; don't settle where you are. There is danger for those that settle. Anyone that settles depreciates. The best option is to keep moving; the best solution is to keep climbing.

To be resolute, you must:

Make a declaration: the number one action to take as you set goals of success is to make a declaration. A declaration states clearly, what you want to achieve as you pursue your goals. A declaration is the proclamation of your vision statement. Any picture of the destination you see in your mind must be openly and emphatically declared. Declaration gives you an extra energy to go for your goals. All modern day organisations have declarations called mission and vision statements. As an individual or a corporate entity, you must also have the same, so that you can daily, see your destination in print and picture. If you mean business about actualising your set goals, make a declaration.

Make a proposition: in an unusual manner, my definition of proposition is prototype; a prototype is a representation. A building contractor about to embark on a major project first designs a prototype before constructing the main building. At prototype stage, corrections and adjustments to designs are made. Apart from that, prototypes are designed plans and presentations that silence doubters. When you set a goal to achieve a certain target in your pursuit, you attract many unbelievers; those who always think impossible. A proposition can help you reduce the number of doubters in your camp; it also gives you something to look forward to. So, create a dummy design of your set goal; don't always leave it in the imaginary; let there be something visible that gives you and people around a clue of where you're going.

Be a determined warrior: it is easy to make plans and construct prototypes because they're all done while sitting on the table in a more comfortable apartment, but when it comes to the nitty-gritty; you've got to get up from the chair and work. It takes determination to work. It takes everything within you to make your dream happen. To make it happen, you have to be unwavering, steadfast, and tenacious. Goals can be set, but if they're not scored, you can't win the game. You didn't sign up to be a loser; you did to be a winner. So, get up and work! Have aims and objectives: aim is the target; objective is the discipline. If you really want to hit the bull's eye, you must be focused and precise. Being specific will help you concentrate all your attention and energy on your uniqueness; your uniqueness must be your aim. Uniqueness makes you become something because you cannot be everything. The challenge most people face is that they want to be everything but end up becoming nothing. So, as you focus, have clear cut objectives; have your rules, guidelines, and roadmap of discipline; these, will form your value system.

Be bold: without boldness, you can't achieve much. Fear is a limitation to someone who wants to rule his world. Cowardice and timidity are retrogressive behaviours that inhibit purposeful achievements. People with trace talents but are bold, can make more progress than those with huge talents but aren't bold. To walk on the terrain of success, you need boldness.

Be consistent: some people begin a project well, but drop out midway. Some people start a pursuit with eagerness, but run out of fuel before its completion. This shouldn't be the attitude of someone that has the intention to succeed. Success requires consistency. Don't stop working until the job is fully done; even when the job is done, set another goal. Setting higher goals keeps you on the driveway, but settling down because a certain target has been achieved makes you park your vehicle on the highway; any vehicle parked on the highway is either a danger or faces danger. Consistency makes you a continuous achiever. Don't stop dreaming; don't stop working; finish it; be consistent!

Be stubborn: to succeed, you need an element of stubbornness. Stubbornness says 'it is possible' when everyone says 'it is impossible'. Stubbornness defies the odds and status quo. Sometimes, to succeed, you must have an element of 'I don't care' attitude. If you're too formal, you'll lose out on a lot of privileges and opportunities. No one will give you bread on a platter of gold for nothing; you must prove that you deserve it; stubbornness gives you that proof. Stubbornness is the indicator that you really need it. Stubbornness is the evidence that you're truly hungry. Be stubborn!

Be perseverant: one night, I had a dream. In that dream, I was hanging on to the outside of the window of a moving bus together with another man; we didn't have a seat inside, but were determined to go with the bus. The driver was driving so fast but we held on. It was very scary!

At one point in the journey, my friend couldn't carry on. So, when the driver slowed down, he jumped off against my advice, and we left him behind. We continued with our journey until we arrived at our destination.

One major definition of perseverance is to uphold. Upholding isn't always easy, but it helps you to persist in anything you undertake. Upholding helps you to maintain a purpose in spite of difficulty, obstacles or discouragement. When you uphold, you continue steadfastly until you reach your destination. My friend in the dream dropped off midway to our destination because of lack of perseverance. You can't reach the place of your dream if you can't be perseverant. No matter the cost, persevere if you truly want to get there.

Interpret your dreams: it is one thing to see a clear picture; it is another to understand the picture. Understanding the picture makes you know, 100% where you're going. If you know where you're going, nothing can turn you back to where you're coming from.

A resolved mind has the message of his dream recorded in the inner recesses of his mind. A resolved mind has the interpretation of the pictures he sees in the file of his heart. It is not possible to keep going when you don't know where you're going. Conviction comes from interpretation. Resolution comes from interpretation.

Be constant: Encyclopedia Britannica says, 'Constant is a number, value, or object that has a fixed magnitude, physically or abstractly, as a part of a specific operation or discussion. In Mathematics the term refers to a quantity that does not change in a certain discussion or operation, or to a variable that assume only one value.'

In other words, constant is a fixed decision; unwavering and unchanging. The mentality of icons to succeed is fixed; it is constant. If you want to be an icon, you must be constant in your decision to stand out in spite of oppositions. Oppositions and distractions walk side by side purposeful endeavours. If you haven't resolved in your heart that despite the storms around you, you are willing and ready to make progress, you will fall by the wayside, not actualised. Constancy is the word for those that are determined to reach the destination of the positive pictures on their minds. One benefit of being constant is that people will know your stand. When people know your stand, they can trust you even if they may not like you. The ability to be trusted, even by perceivable enemies is a great attribute in life and pursuits. Never change your mind when you put your hand on the plough. Let your heart and mind maintain the value and objective of excellence. It may take a while, but if you insist, you will succeed!

Be courageous: courage is inner strength, power, or quality of mind or spirit that enables a person to face difficulty, danger or pains with or without fear. I added 'with or without fear' because someone may be afraid, but yet continue moving. For me, that is super courage; the ability to defy fear.

It takes courage to make some leadership decisions. Courage is required when taking some leadership and visionary actions. Stepping into certain markets need courage because you're not sure whether you'll succeed or not. Going into certain careers or professions require courage. There is nothing purposeful or heading somewhere great that doesn't have the need of courage.

When do you begin to gather the courage to take certain actions? My answer is that courage begins as you take the first step, and grows as you continue taking more steps. If you sit down to have enough courage before making that move, you may never find it. Making the move in spite of your fears is what generates the courage to accomplish the set target.

Be dauntless: dauntlessness is refusal to be intimidated. As you walk or run on the lane of destiny, many issues and unforeseen circumstances that appear gigantic will spontaneously confront you. It is your refusal to bow to these bullies that will create the access route to your destination. Be dauntless. Refuse to bow to mountainous cowards. They look big, but are actually inflated balloons. Burst your way through, and forge into the life you were born to live. Fear not the obstacles that oppose progress. You were born to win; you were born to succeed. Be daring, be brave, and be indomitable!

Be dedicated: the ability to devote oneself wholly to a special purpose is dedication. Dreams come true by devotion. Visions manifest by dedication.

I read the story of Spencer West from sobadsogood.com. At the age of 5, Spencer tragically lost both legs. In spite of not having legs, the Canadian was determined to get to the top of Mount Kilimanjaro. He spent 12 months in intensive training, making sure his arms and hands were strong enough to support the extreme physical pressure they'd be put under. It took him a gruelling 7 days to make it to the summit. He travelled only using his hands for a stunning 80% of the trek, with his two friends willing him on. As a result of his action, he raised £300 000 for Free the children charity!

While most so called able bodied men can't climb ten floors of a building, the one considered less-able, did the unimaginable through the character of dedication.

Dedication comes from being resolute. Dedication is offspring of commitment and determination. All icons are dedicated people; they die for what they believe. To be an icon, be dedicated to your vision and calling. To be an icon, let your dedication defy your obstacles and limitations. To be an icon, let your dedication surpass your inabilities, incapacities, and disabilities.

Be energetic: energy operates on three levels; spiritual, mental and physical. You need all of them to help you achieve success in your pursuit. Physical strength, without a mental one wouldn't take you anywhere. There are certain encounters you can't overwhelm with your physical strength alone. Without mental energy, you will wear out and abandon your dream on the highway of life. The reason being that, life's greatest pressures are on the mind; except the mind has enough will to cope, it will crack and crumble. Many people that committed suicides, did, because their mental strengths were suspects.

Once upon a time, in the city of London, with a wife and two little children, I was homeless and jobless because the system wanted to choke me up. Throughout the 12 months of my ordeal, the major thought that kept bugging my mind was suicide. I looked at the implication from all ramifications, and decided that the best option was to live. I decided that I will live for my wife and children, even if the condition says die. It took a lot of spiritual and mental energy to counter that voice of hopelessness.

To deal with hopelessness, you must be energetic. Icons are energetic. Be an icon.

Be firm: on this subject, I am not approaching firmness from the angle of steadiness, constancy or determination, but from the level of organisation. Realise that a firm also means an organised enterprise or business. A resolve that does not have a goal, objective or target dissipates useful energy in fruitlessness. Therefore, to be resolute, you must be business minded. Business mindedness helps you to achieve something tangible and notable. If a pursuit does not have an end point, it is useless and fruitless. So, the question is where does your dream begin and end? For every race, there is a finish line. No athlete in all honesty wants to run forever. And no athlete in all honesty wants to run for nothing. Anyone that pursues a dream must have the hope of substance and end point.

One of the topics I taught my students when I was a chemistry teacher was volumetric analysis. Volumetric analysis involves titration of one solution against another. For example, a certain quantity of acid can be titrated against a certain quantity of base. Before doing acid-base titration, you must use an indicator. An indicator acts like a referee; it tells you when you get to the end point. When a drop of indicator is added to a base, it helps change the colour of the base. But at the end point, that colour changes to pink. This gives you an idea of when to stop the titration.

No one can be resolute for what he doesn't know its end. That is why firmness is relevant. Firmness gives a defined structure. Firmness tells you your beginning and destination. Firmness is organisation. Be firm. Be organised. Be an icon!

Have the gut: gut is audacity. Audacity makes you daring. Audacity is effrontery. Audacity is impertinence, brashness and impudence.

Before I began my writing career, my mind played a foul game on me. He told me that if I write, no one would buy because I am unknown. He further told me that the big authors have written everything and that there was nothing else I would say, that they haven't said. At first, I believed that voice, until my wife helped push me into the lane to compete. As I began, I said to myself, *'they may have written everything but wouldn't definitely write it using my approach because every writer has his uniqueness, and no one can say it using my own genetics.'* Due to this resolution, I summoned the gut to step out and air my view whether some people like it or not. When I began, the first enemies I had were those that should have been friends and supporters. That was my first shocker or maybe, I should call it baptism of fire, but that didn't deter me. Rather than stop, I went further to become a daily blogger, and that even infuriated some *'friends'*; I mean fiends. Then I realised that the most difficult pain to heal as you head towards your vision is the one inflicted on you by those who know you. These are people who feel that you shouldn't be the one to take the stage. But to take that stage, you must have guts. If you don't, you won't go far in your pursuits. Icons have lots of guts. Don't let anyone stop you. Don't look at their faces to decide how far you'll go. Carry on with the chase, and soon, you'll become an ace.

Have intent: intent is the foundation, background and originality of purpose. Without it, you can't design or paint the picture of your destination.

Success must have intent, otherwise, it won't happen. No one succeeds by luck. No one succeeds by accident. Success comes by purpose. Success comes by design. Success comes by intention.

To succeed, you must adopt the principles of success. You need those principles in the locker room of your innermost heart. Having them alone can't help you; you must daily brood on them and adopt them as your daily standard of living. This is what produces the right intent within you. This is what challenges you to surpass mediocrity. This is what forms the skeleton of your life, and the backbone of your wisdom.

As you walk on the road, your intent becomes the succession of imaginations rolling like a film tape in your inner being. This succession of imagination becomes your dream.

Dream your intent. Believe your intent. Work on your intent. Make a positive change.

Make the right judgment: when I come in contact with the word judgment, I always recall what President Barack Obama said about President George Bush's decision to invade Iraq. He said George Bush made an error of judgment. It means in other words that judgment is connected, not just with verdicts from the court, but leadership decisions.

94

Making the right judgment requires a lot of courage because some quality decisions will hurt your folks, and even those that are loyal to you. On certain occasions, making the right judgment might even go against you, but if it is right, great leadership suggests that you should make it. If you make it, you succeed, but if you let sentiment dominate you, you fail in that area of your life. If you fail in an area that is very sensitive, it might hurt you for life.

What is right is right. What isn't right isn't right. It takes courage and right judgment to know this. You can't be an icon without understanding this principle. Emotion can be demotion if we don't know when and where to stop accelerating the motion. Be sensible; make quality decisions; make right judgments.

Be obstinate: obstinacy makes you overcome obstacles rather than being overcome. With obstinacy, you control your destiny rather than leaving it in the hands of other people. An obstinate person won't allow anyone to lure him out of the lane of progress even if the immediate circumstances don't suggest positivity. So, don't be paper weight to the winds blowing against your progress; be obstinate.

When you're obstinate, some people may consider you stubborn or arrogant, but insist on being in charge of your destiny. Don't relinquish leadership to those interested in driving you on the road of misfit. Stand your ground; be in charge.

Be relentless: relentlessness is tirelessness. A relentless person never draws back from taking purposeful actions. A relentless person never makes excuses for not advancing towards the place of vision. A relentless person is workaholic.

For a marathon athlete, what makes him complete the race is the ability not to yield to physical and mental pains. To a boxer in a fierce fight, what makes him not to surrender is his adamant and unbending attitude. Due to this, he goes ahead to win the fight.

If you want to win, be relentless. If you want your vision to actualise, be relentless. If you want your dream to go beyond the night season, be relentless.

Icons are relentless. Be an icon!

CHAPTER FIVE

FOCUS, KEENNESS, AND PRECISION

One way of identifying icons is their focus, keenness, and precision. These three qualities make anyone with a dream invaluable. What are they?

FOCUS

In darts for instance, the player requires a lot of focus to hit the bull's eye. In life as well, to succeed, focus is one of the most essential requirements. What distinguishes an icon is focus. In goal setting, focus is a major key that helps you win. With focus, you can beat any opponent; with focus, you can defeat any opposition.

Sometime ago, I was in the studio section of a conference airing a live television programme. My reason for being there was because I couldn't get a seat in the main hall as it was jam packed. While there, I began to notice and learn some life changing principles. I totally believe that principles are the laws of change; so I always embrace them when I find them. As I sat behind the Mixing Engineer, there was one word he kept repeating in almost every statement as he communicated with the Cameramen. I would hear him say, '*Camera one, improve your focus. Camera two, your focus is blurred, zoom out. Camera three, focus on the man with the white shirt'*. All through the programme, it was focus, focus, and focus.

What is focus? Focus is the central point of attraction, attention, and activity; focus is the place of concentration, convergence, and spotlight. In essence, focus is the ability to see one thing, hear one thing, and follow one thing. The problem with a lot of people is that they see, hear, and follow too many things. As a result, they end up nothing. You can only end up something when you see one thing. Seeing too many things makes you see nothing. There are people who study too many things and end up in confusion. To make a difference in life, you don't need too many things. If you are not specific, you cannot be an expert. If you are not specific, you cannot be a specialist. I have heard or probably met people who are Medical Doctors and qualified Accountants at the same time. Such people boast of their qualifications, but if you take a closer look, you will discover that they are always in second positions in both careers; they're hardly first. If you don't put your eyes on one thing, and pursue it to the utmost, you will remain feeble and fickle. To be the best, you must be focused. Life without focus is life without form; life without focus is life without future. If you do not focus, you will be off-course. Being off-course is diverting or deviating from a set target; diverting or deviating from set target is derailment. No sensible person wants to join a train that is bound to derail. Derailment is tantamount to death; it is the quickest way to aborting a purposeful vision.

What you see, study, and work on daily, can easily be manipulated, innovated, or recreated. Understanding is the key to creativity. You cannot pursue three things at the same time and expect to know the details of those three things 100%. To be focused, you must make a choice. Your choice must go with your passion. I must make you understand that passion does not always bring instant hit; most choices made by passion require endurance before the dividends begin to manifest. In every focus, there's a price to pay; when you pay it, you later gain it. It may take time, but focused people end up winning.

If you're not known for one thing, no one will trust you. I cannot hand a responsibility to someone who is Jack of all trades because, I can't tell how much he knows. Knowing a bit of everything doesn't make you an expert in anything. For creativity to be effective there must be specificity. As a person with a Biochemistry background, I know that enzymes are specific. Each enzyme digests only one type of food. For this reason, one molecule of enzyme can digest hundreds of thousands of molecules of its specific kind of food. Youachieve so much in your area of choice if you are focused. Focus gives direction. Focus produces confidence. Focus makes a person an authority. No one will ask you to autograph what you did not create; you can only create what you focus on. Sometime ago, I spoke in a conference in United Kingdom about Purpose based on one of my Books; Finding Real Purpose. As attendees were purchasing copies of the Book, most of them insisted that I have to autograph their copies. If I had not been specific or focused in my area of calling, I wouldn't be able to author a book in that area. You cannot write about what you're not focused on.

Being everything and everywhere means going to and fro, back and forth; it means working but not making progress. Progress is achieved by focus; progress is attained by concentration. For the fact a man is sweating does not mean he's advancing; advancement is gained by taking purposeful steps in a specific direction; not directions. Attempting to walk on two or more roads at the same time is equivalent to tearing yourself to pieces. If you're in pieces, you can't have peace. Where there is no peace, there is no feast. Be specific; see one thing. The power to excel is in the power of focus. Focused people end up as famous people!

To be focused, what do you need to do?

You must have a target point: your target point is your goal. Focusing without a goal is tantamount to madness. A man by a roadside, standing still, staring, but at nothing needs a Psychiatric attention.

Your goal is your expected result. Your goal is your reason for exerting all your energy into work. No goal, no purpose.

The dream of every visionary is to win something excellent at the end of walking on a tedious road. No one should be on the road of a vision merely for a hobby; hobbies pay no dividend. Focus on a fruitful target. Waste no time focusing on things with little or no value.

You must have a great vision: if you have no eyes, no matter how much you focus, you cannot see. Even if you have eyes, if they're myopic, you cannot see properly; myopia is short sightedness.

The ability to see beyond today is great vision. The ability to see beyond the immediate is great vision. Great vision separates great leaders from mere managers. Great vision builds for today and the future, but managers only coordinate what leaders build.

You must have illumination: illumination is light; light is information. Good eyesight without light makes you grope in the dark. Many people can see, but because they're in the dark, their good vision means nothing to them. Good vision easily manifest in environments of exposure. Without light, anything hidden in secret cannot be exposed. There are lots of talented children in developing countries, but their environments limit them. For this reason, some footballers who were not discovered on time almost pass their useful ages because no one saw them to know their depth of talent. Some talented singers die unnoticed because no one shined the light on them.

Focus requires illumination. Illumination is information, knowledge and exposure. Illumination could be a person who knows how to help you sharpen, redirect, harness, groom, and market your talent. Best vision is equivalent to no vision if you're in the dark.

You must have a great head: a great head is a great leader. When I talk about a great leader, I'm not referring to some great world known leader, dead or alive. I am talking about that mentor that may not be known even in your street; that person that encourages you often, and counsels you on how to keep being excellent in your pursuit. I am also talking about the author of that book you always run to; that book that helps you sharpen your gift, and helps you to keep pushing when everything turns against you.

Remember, your vision or eyes are situated on your head. Without head, there are no eyes. If your eyes are located on your chest, then, you're an evil monster. You need a great head to have a great focus. If you have no head, you have no life!

You must have a strong but flexible neck: the neck holds the head; the eyes are located on the head. The neck connects the head with the rest of the body. Without the rest of the body, the vision cannot function.

Relationship is a key to focusing. You can't succeed in isolation. You can't excel in isolation, no matter how great your vision is. To network with vital people, you must have an outgoing personality. Your outgoing personality must be flexible like the neck, so that it will be able to turn to different directions. People in different directions have different qualities that are needed by your vision. Your vision is in need of these people in order to get to its destination.

101

You must have the right skill and tools: focus without skill is outrageously nonsensical. If you haven't learnt how to shoot an arrow, it is impossible for you to aim and bring down an antelope at a considerable distance. Skill is required in focus.

To sharpen your skill, you must keep practising. To practise, you require the tools. Tools are knowledge. Regular application of knowledge obtained from your skills helps you develop into the dimension of wisdom. At wisdom level, skills head towards perfection.

You must be self motivated: when focusing on a pursuit, the conditions aren't always right. You must learn to adapt. Some conditions will be hazy, chilly or foggy, or maybe, a combination of all of them, but you must be ready to cope. To cope, you need to be self motivated. The best motivation that will help you stand the test of time and the environment is the one you give to yourself. In a vision, there are days of shades and Hades, you must be ready to withstand the fiery furnace without burning if you really want the promotion you seek. Challenge yourself to continue with the race when all say it is unachievable. Inspire yourself to drive on, when the fuel in your tank has been completely exhausted. Jump out of the vehicle if it breaks down, and continue with the journey till you get to the true place of rest. Don't stop; be inspired; be self motivated.

KEENNESS

Sometime ago, I watched a short documentary on the bald eagle. I was so amazed about how keen the eagle is. I have heard so much about the focus of the eagle, but have never really taken the time to ruminate on its keenness. As I pondered on it, I started comparing the keenness of the eagle with the skills of man. My conclusion was that if man possesses the mentality of the eagle, his skills will be better, deeper and more productive.

What is a skill? Skill involves ability, knowledge, practice and aptitude. It also involves competent excellence in performance, expertness and dexterity. The more man digs into knowledge, the more he becomes skilful in his chosen endeavour. But the challenge for man is that most people prefer to remain at the periphery of wisdom, and as a result, their level of knowledge becomes obsolete, dated or scanty. To keep with the flow, or remain relevant, updates must be daily uptakes, and uptakes must be daily intakes. What you consume daily is what determines your growth level. We don't just grow in physical size; we also grow in our mentalities. Physical height has its maximum size but mental growth is ongoing. That is why we must follow the dynamics, if we really want our skills to go beyond history.

The following reasons are why skills require keenness:

Keenness produces a sharpened cutting edge skill: some innovations don't require dynamites to crack them; all they need is sharpened knife edge to cut them. If you always come with dynamites, you will destroy what you're trying to create. Making a statue out of wood needs a sharp knife edge to fine tune your creativity; you don't need explosives to do that. So, keenness produces the common sense of wisdom that helps cut through obstacles and debacles; in every skill, there are obstacles and debacles.

Keenness produces a piercing skill: for a nurse to inject a patient, she doesn't need to cut through the skin; she only needs to pierce the skin with the needle. In a skill, there is a cutting stage and a piercing stage. Don't pierce when you should cut, and don't cut when you should pierce. Sometimes, oil explorers, rather than cut, pierce. The reason for piercing is to get the treasures from remote areas, impossible for most eyes to see. As you sharpen your skills, remember to make its pointed end prick.

103

Keenness produces a biting skill: in the human mouth, there are different types of teeth. It consists of incisor, canine, molars and premolars. Each type has its own function; for cutting, tearing, chewing or grinding. Your skill must have the ability to bite, tear, cut, and grind.

The marketplace is highly competitive; if you don't have teeth, you can't take your share. So, your skill must have teeth. There isn't a gentleman in the marketplace; everyone wants to sell; everyone wants to win. You can only have something substantial if you have a biting skill. Keenness gives you that biting skill.

Keenness produces distinctive perception: one major attribute that many career and professional people have ignored is perception. Perception is what differentiates the leaders from the led. Perception is intuitiveness, insight and discernment. Perception helps you to recognise immediately what hasn't yet taken place. It is the element behind being proactive.

The ability to study the market and immediately see what other people can't see makes your skill distinctively perceptive. The ability to see the picture of innovation that other people can't behold makes you creative. Without perception, creativity becomes illusion. Keenness produces perception; go for it.

Keenness produces eagerness or enthusiasm: you have no right to dream if you're not eager or enthusiastic about your dream. Enthusiasm is a driving force that takes you to your dreamland. Eagerness is the hunger that makes you realise that until you reach the place you see in your innermost heart, your present location will keep hunting or hurting you.

If you aren't keen, you can't advance. Keenness in your skill sends you into the class of continuous personal development.Being satisfied where you are isn't an attitude of keen people. So, be eager to get out of where you are, and head towards where you should be.

Keenness gives mental penetration, intense desire, and the ambition to succeed in your pursuits. Keenness is characterised by strength, extreme sensitivity and responsiveness. In your skill, be keen. In your career, be keen. In your profession, be keen. In your life, be seriously keen!

PRECISION

Focus and keenness help you to be precise. Definition is important in precision because it sets forth the meaning of your destination. When you understand the meaning of your goal, you become strict on scoring that goal. Hitting that target requires accuracy, because the consequences of missing certain targets are devastating. For instance, if your target is to hit a lion, imagine what it will be like if you miss. The same thing applies to certain goals that are set; missing is very consequential. If you are investing on a high risk business with a lot of money, your target is to make profit. If you miss that target, you are in serious palaver. That is why precision is extremely essential; you must never get it wrong.

Some people have lost their jobs because they missed the target. There is zero tolerance for missing certain targets; no sentiment is welcome. If you hit it, you win all; if you miss it, you lose all. So, it is undoubtedly essential to understand how to shoot without missing.

In weather forecasts for instance, it may be tolerable to get some mild weather changes wrong, but getting it wrong on issues like tsunami or hurricane is unacceptable. Some people in life have misfired in their destinies, which is inexcusable.

105

Some parents for instance, have carelessly miscalculated their decisions and actions relating to the future of their children, and as a result, messed up their tomorrow; you must be accurate on issues of life and death. Issues of life and death are issues of dreams, visions, purpose, and destiny.

If the archer can hit his target, you have no excuse not to. If the golfer can hit the ball, and take it into the hole, you can do the same with life and pursuit. If the bowler in one throw can bring all the pins down, there's no reason why you shouldn't pursue your dream with clear cut motive, enthusiasm and drive, in order to achieve the best results. You must be precise is your endeavour.

It is possible to be explicit, specific and absolute. It is possible to carve out a defined standard that will produce the required success. It is possible to hit that precision that will make you a champion. Be precise!

To be precise, you need to have discipline, restraint, and patience. Discipline, restraint, and patience help you wait for the right time before shooting. If you fire in haste, you will lose your game. Sometimes, you may not only lose your game, but your chance or maybe, your life. So, show that discipline of someone heading towards a purposeful destination. Show that restraint of a cautious hunter. Display the patience of an aged woman that has seen it all. Don't take off before the umpire says so, otherwise, you'll be disqualified. Wait for the right time; be precise.

Sometime ago, someone made a serious allegation about financial fraud regarding some people, and she was about taking the issue up without proper investigation. When she told me, I advised her to get the facts right before blowing it out, because if she misses it, the consequences will spell a devastating doom. Why I told her that was because precision is a key to identification.

106

Before you shoot, do a research. Never fire without a perfect understanding. If you're investing, do a research. If you're to be invested upon, also research the financier. Whatever deal or pursuit you're going into, research must be number one element of being precise. If you have not found out, don't waste your arrow. If you do, you'll lose a vital weapon that should have given you a greater value.

Researchers come up with different methods of doing things. Among the different methods, one or two may be suitable. So, when you research, you must pick the best approach suitable for you. Don't pick an approach based on its suitability for another person, because what is good for another may not be for you. Your approach must suit your uniqueness. Hit your target with your uniqueness!

When you find your approach, go for it. Waste no time when you discover your uniqueness. Wait for no one when you find your identity. It is better to shoot when the time and approach are right. Don't delay when you should be on the lane. Run the mile; run the distance. Fire the shot; hit the bull's eye. Be precise!

CHAPTER SIX

POSITIONING, DIRECTION, AND DESTINATION

To be an icon, you must understand the concepts of positioning, direction, and destination. It will change your perception about life, if you do.

POSITIONING

In positioning, you don't always wait for things to come to you; you go to where the things are, and where they're happening. This means that positioning is a deliberate decision to succeed. We are not always lucky; if we were, everyone would win lotteries. Life may be a game of chance sometimes, but it isn't, always. Most successes aren't achieved by chance; they are, through readiness, willingness, and purposeful decisions. If this is the case, it means that by personal devise, a man can either succeed or fail. It depends on where he positions himself.

Simply put, positioning is being at the right place at the right time. For instance, when you and your bus arrive at the bus stop the same time; that is considered to be perfect timing. So, positioning is best defined as the meeting point between preparedness and opportunity.

Your positioning determines how you are perceived. You are a brand; the way and manner you package yourself is the way the world will accept you. The price people are willing and ready to place on you is determined by how and where you place yourself. Your value is dictated by your positioning.

Your talent, gift, product or service is a brand. Its ability to solve a problem, meet a need, or provide benefits to its users helps position it. Positioning isn't just jumping into the marketplace; at the end of the day, it is all about perception. Whoever perceives you, will receive you, conceive you, or deceive you. If you are received, it means you have met the need. If you are conceived, there may be a future plan to patronise you, but if you're deceived, it means they aren't bold enough to tell you that your offering is crap. That is why you must be well positioned from start to finish before ending up in the marketplace. Choosing a market niche or being in a target market does not mean you're well positioned. Positioning must have a strong foundation before ever venturing into unknown location.

I must reaffirm that branding has gone beyond physical products. Your calling, dreams and visions are brands. Your career or profession is a brand. Your gift or talent is a brand. Therefore, the first brand to position in life is you. If you can't properly position yourself, you can't excellently position a product. It is the understanding of self positioning that metamorphous into great product positioning. People that can, or have properly positioned themselves make great leaders. People that were also properly positioned also make great leaders. For example, some parents combine great education and discipline in raising their children. Most of these children have ended up becoming some of the world's greatest leaders in government, business and social enterprises; all because one thoughtful parent or parents decided to do the right thing.

110

What do you require before positioning? I believe that in order to properly position, one needs to:

Have foresight: foresight is prevision, prescience, and provision for the future. Foresight gives one the ability to look forward and act forward. For instance, during the London 2012 Olympic Games, everyone was expecting that the person that will light the torch will be one almighty celebrity, but to everyone's surprise, the organisers used some unknown young athletes; the reason for doing that was because they were thinking into the future, and handing the future over to those that own it; the youth.

To rightly position, you must see ahead of your current situation, and take actions that surpass your current situation. Accepting the limitations of your present circumstance cannot place you where you should be.

Where do you want to be in the next 5, 10, 15, or 20 years? You should know now; if you don't, you can't begin working towards where you don't have your sight on. Foresight looks ahead. Foresight sees into the future and prepares for the future.

Have foreknowledge: some people see where they're going but never take the time to study where they're going. Foreknowledge is knowledge before destination. Before stepping into your target destination, you must find out about where you're going. Finding out gives you information on how to engage and interact with your expected destination or position. Success cannot accommodate those that don't understand her. For instance, there are certain lottery winners that ended up seriously broke after a few years of having some free millions of dollars in their accounts. Most of them went back to the pit of poverty because when they stepped into the city of success, they weren't prepared, neither did they, as they got there, have the wisdom to quickly learn about their new environment. So, many didn't know how to, or

111

where to make purposeful investments. Rather than plant the money, they ate the seeds because they didn't realise that money is a seed meant to be planted in the ground called investment. Because they ate their seeds, they ended up going hungry.

In all your endeavours, you must have foreknowledge. Foreknowledge advises you on what to do, and what not to. No prudent businessman or organisation with good leadership will venture into an unknown land without prior understanding of where they're going. Unfortunately, some people or businesses have taken miscalculated risks based on hearsay, sparse, or empty information. I know a footballer that signed a life contract with a team when African players were just beginning to make it into European leagues. He didn't seek relevant information from experts; he signed away his life. By the time he realised it, he was too old to take his case to FIFA.

Foreknowledge is a major decision in positioning. Don't joke with it.

Understand the concept of right timing: there is an African artiste; a great performer with a golden voice like that of nightingale. His name is Majek Fashek; a rock-reggae musician that sings with a wailing and emotional voice. In the late eighties, he released an LP titled, 'Send down the rain'. In those days, most times, when he performed on stage, it does actually rain. People always attributed the rains to his song; so, they tagged him, the rainmaker. I have no doubt that music connects with nature and spirituality, but what happened was that the music company that signed him on, released his album during the rainy season in order to give it that connection. As a result, most times that he was promoting his debut album, it would rain. So, in addition to his lovely voice, timing was very useful in positioning him.

You can have a great talent, product or service, but if you can't time its release, you will make it look insignificant. Most fashion retail shops don't sell winter clothes in summer because they will have very little number of footfalls. Time must be connected with need. If it's not needed, it isn't yet time.

Understand the dynamics of different locations: I live in England, and since I relocated, I have never one day given a damn about Clark Shoes, because in my opinion, there are other good shoe retailers. But I dare not say this in Jamaica. In Jamaica, Clark Shoes are comparable to gold. The brand is seriously revered. Since this is the case, what should Clark Shoes management do? Of course, litter Jamaica with its brand.

Another brand I will like to mention is Primark. For one reason or the other, for years, I haven't stepped into Primark to buy anything for myself or family. But when my brother in-law visited from Nigeria, his friends and family members were calling frequently to demand specifically for Primark products. If I were Primark Chief Executive, I will see that as an opportunity for business expansion for a population that is about three times as big as Britain.

What I am trying to say in essence is that timing for different locations differs. What is untimely in one location may be timely in another. That is why it is necessary that in positioning, you must look beyond your immediate environment. It may be summer in United Kingdom, but winter in South Africa. It may be day in Egypt but night in United States. Understanding the dynamics of locations will help you understand how and when to position yourself, brand, or any other pursuit.

Understand the significance of growth and development: individually or corporately, everyone must realise the essence of growth and development. In positioning, you don't just walk into it; you grow into it. A child that is born today does not walk into adulthood; she grows into

113

adulthood. Sometimes, I see certain people that want to jump the gun, and I do feel for them because jumping the gun gets you disqualified. Some people have disqualified themselves because they refused the meals that should make them grow. Growth meals don't always taste nice, especially the meals that well position visions. Due to this, many people avoid them, and preferably go for things that are tasty but deadly. To be well positioned, you must follow the process of growth.

Some people grow but don't develop. Development helps you look for new methods of improvement; it is a product of continuous research. The product that is the toast of town, yesterday, definitely wouldn't be, today. To keep up with the competition or even have a competitive advantage, you must keep growing; continuous growth is development. If you don't develop, you'll be overtaken by infants. Then, you will start talking about the good old days. If you have to keep relying on history to prove your relevance, you're dated!

Be Prepared: talent is not preparation; it is a gift. You can be talented but if not prepared, your talent will end up a raw material; you can't put crude oil in a tank of a car; it will knock the engine. One of the worst crimes a man can commit against his vision, dream, purpose, and destiny is for opportunity to knock on his door when his either ill-prepared or not prepared at all. The unfortunate thing is that most people are caught in the web of lack of preparation, yet, they keep asking for privileges. Privileges are caps that fit the heads of prepared people. There's someone I know that had the opportunity to be appointed to a position of being a representative of a government, but he was semi-educated. He had every chance to upgrade himself, but chose to remain on the same level. When the position for elevation called, he was found wanting. Preparation

114

is the development that pushes you to the level of opportunities. Opportunities are always up, it takes those who go up to reach them; preparation takes you up.

Be consistent in and with what you do: consistency is the degree of density, firmness, and viscosity. Consistency is steadfast adherence to disciplined and winning principles, forms, or course. Consistency is synonymous to reliability, continuation, and coherence with creative principles. There is every need to form the habit of continuity in what you are designed to do; everyone was designed to fulfil an assignment. When you embark on your design, don't do it like it's a hobby. Every design was drawn to create a product of legacy. To make something of legacy, the character of consistency is required. Consistency positions a man for success. A talented man who is not consistent in pruning his talent will end up in a raw state. An intellectual who is inconsistent in updating himself will be outdated. A businessman who is inconsistent with prevailing business and marketing ideas will go bankrupt. Consistency is a product of hard work; consistency is a product of self discipline. No one can properly position himself if he is inconsistent with the principles inclined to his calling, vision, or purpose.

Take advantage of opportunities: opportunities come in different shapes, forms, colours, and sizes. Some people identify them; some don't. There are people sleeping and waking up with opportunities but cannot identify them. There are people dining and wining with opportunities but do not realise it. A man cannot identify what he cannot see; a man cannot take advantage of what he cannot behold. Opportunities are rough and sometimes very dirty. Opportunities appear insignificant most times. Opportunities sometimes, speak with the voice of lack of seriousness; this voice appears passive a times. If you're not sensitive, you cannot take advantage of what should add immense

115

value to your life. Problems are opportunities that help people break into new information. Problems are privileges begging for new forms of research. Problems are not always hazards. If you see every situation as an opportunity to create a positive difference, you will succeed in every endeavour of your life. Take advantage of opportunities; be sensitive to opportunities.

You must deliver: some people are given opportunities but cannot deliver. To deliver means to do or carry out an assigned responsibility as promised. Sometime ago, I was in a workshop where someone was given an opportunity to make a presentation. When he was introduced, he was hiding behind the sound engineers; I was shocked. When he finally took over the microphone, he was dithering and shivering. In my opinion, the presentation was flawed. If you take advantage of an opportunity, please deliver. If you don't deliver, you won't be recalled.

Again, you must realise that success is not coincidence; it is a deliberate determination to step out of the ordinary. Success is not an accident; if it was, all successful people will be in their graves. To succeed, you must obey the laws of success; one of the laws of success is proper positioning. If you want to be successful, you must put yourself in the location of successful people. Location is not always geographical; it is sometimes non-geographical. Positioning is not always in form of physical boundaries; it is mainly developmental. Develop yourself; grow yourself by acquiring and constantly developing the skills necessary for your calling. Exhibit the right characters, and you will succeed.

DIRECTION

It is possible to know where you want to be, but if you don't know how to get there, you may be stuck where you are. Where you want to be is your destination but to know how to get there, you need direction.

How can you get to the place you want to be? What should you do in order to be there? Knowing your direction is what will take you to your destination. Direction involves:

Making quality decisions: in life and pursuits, you must first decide where you're going. If you do not, you'll go nowhere, go anywhere, or go everywhere. If you go nowhere, you'll remain redundant. If you go anywhere, you're aimless. If you go everywhere, you don't understand your purpose. Making quality decisions on direction will help you narrow down where you should be, and how to reach the place of your ultimate decision.

Decision is the strongest part of direction. In decision making, you must have a made-up mind that you want to reach somewhere, and then begin planning on how you'll get to the place. Without proper decision making, you'll either remain confused or don't have a clue whether life requires a move from your current location.

The need for a road map: a road map is a plan or guide of how to get to your destination; without it, you'll be lost. Without a road map, you can't know your route. If you don't have a road map, you can't determine the distance of your journey and how much it will cost you to get there. Road map is useful for budgeting and strategic planning. Apart from planning and budgeting, no vision minded person will take you serious when you don't have a map of your life's destination.

As a leader, where is your road map? If you don't have one, you may lead your people astray. As an entrepreneur, where is your road map? Without one, you'll get stuck on the highway. As a student, parent, or career or professional person, you need a road map to succeed in your endeavours. No roadmap, no direction.

Circumstantial eyes: some people can see tomorrow but are blind to today. Some people can tell the future but can't tell where they are. There are chief executive officers with great visions and strategies to move their companies to where they should be, but are ignorant of the plights of the common people working for their organisations. Some people are so disconnected from their environments, while even achieving global milestones. If you can't take care of the immediate, even if you take care of the future, you're not a complete success. If you can't take care of your home, even if you take care of a nation, you aren't fully successful yet. You need to see what is around you, in order to take purposeful steps into where you want to be. If you can't see your street, how can you walk to the bus or train station? If you always need the help of another person to lead you out of your immediate circumstance, I don't care if you've killed lions; you still have a long way to go. Some people build cities but can't build a home.

Direction requires you to see where you are now. Don't be blind to your current location even if you're heading to a better location. If you can't recognise where you are, you can't tell how to get out. People who can't tell their locations are taken advantage of. Some junior employees have put some senior employees into trouble because some managers are too busy doing big things, that they ignore the elementary things. Elementary things make up the building blocks of organisations. If you ignore them, you'll bring down the company. Some parents also are busy making big money, until the teenager got pregnant.

If your eyes can't see the now, it will get to the future brutalised. If you're undiscerning or insensitive to your immediate environment, you may still make it to the next level, but not with the people you were planning to take along. Open your eyes and see where you are. Don't be blind to today. Have a circumstantial eye; have intuitive and discerning eyes.

The need for a navigator: life has gone beyond prints on papers; software rules in our current dispensation. Maps are now on mobile communication gadgets. We have maps that talk; it is the navigator.

As a leader or intending leader, never mess with the power of intuition. Intuition is a lifetime navigator that will show you the right route to your destination. Intuition will help you know intentions or deceptions. Intuition is a product of your human spirit. If you develop it, it will direct and alert you. Intuition is perceptive recognition of what your five senses cannot understand. It is that inner feeling that you cannot literarily explain.

For a month after the demise of my twin brother, my family members were scared of telling me because of the impact it will have on me. But, on the day he died, intuitively, I knew. I even told one of my mates that my twin brother has died; without me hearing from anyone. I just perceived it in my human spirit. Again, sometimes, if I am having a discussion with someone, no matter how honest and subtle the person may appear, intuitively, I will know whether the person is lying or not. Intuition directs you, guides you or navigates you, so that you won't make regrettable decisions.

You don't only need a physical guide; you also need a spiritual guide. Don't be ignorant.

The need for people: when you travel on a road, sometimes, in spite of having maps and navigators, you can still miss your way. At this point, you need people. Most people you meet on the road to your destination are unknown to you, yet, they're relevant to you. If you don't want to keep gyrating on the highway, respect those you meet on the highway. On the highway, you need to be polite. On the highway, you must understand the relevance of excellent communication skills. On the highway, you must climb down from your high horse

119

to ask for the direction to your destiny. If you don't behave on the highway, you will miss your way, waste useful time, or get stuck. Many are stuck on their way to their destination. Many have also died on that road, with unfulfilled dreams.

The need for signposts: signposts are not humans, but they are written, designed, and fixed by humans. You may not find anyone on the highway, but if you follow the signposts, you can't miss your way. Signposts are relevant information required for your direction. They are short, bold and precise. They may not be written words, but signs that point to where you should go. So, you must understand signs if you want to reach your place of expectation because information come in words, signs and symbols. As short as certain information may be, they will lead, guide, instruct and direct you to your place of purpose. Don't ignore signposts.

A signpost may be a word spoken by someone that doesn't know you; maybe, the word wasn't even meant for you, but you knew its relevance in your life, so, you took it and used it, and it worked for you. A signpost may be an update posted by someone on the social media or an article written by someone online or print media, but was relevant to you. It could also be an advice given to you by someone, or the content of a book you read, CD you listened to, or DVD you watched. To the designer of the signpost, it may just be another update or post, but to you, it is a direction to your destination. So, don't ignore signposts!

The need for a vehicle: you can't always walk to your destination; you may have to drive, sail, or fly depending on the distance. If you can't on your own, drive, sail, or fly, you must pay the fares. Even if you can drive, sail, or fly, you also incur costs. The costs you incur may be too high if you drive, sail, or fly alone. But if you have passenger seats, charging for driving them will help alleviate the costs. In short, if you're wise, you'll make profits. Driving, sailing, or flying requires skills. You can't drive without learning how to. It is far less expensive, if you arm yourself with relevant skills as you move towards your destiny. Movement without skill makes the journey too expensive.

The need to follow the rules: every drive has rules. If you don't follow the rules, you'll have an accident. As you drive, realise that speed kills. As you drive, take cognisance of other road users. If you drive carelessly, you won't reach your destination. As you follow your direction, caution is the watch word. Never drive in the opposite direction to your destination; follow your lane; follow your goal. Don't drive in the opposite direction of your goal if you don't want to score an own goal; don't also drive outside your goal. Don't copy those that are in haste; life isn't a competition. The only competition as far as purpose and destiny are concerned is you against you. Those in haste don't like going through driving lessons. They hate to take the test; so, they never passed any test. They put themselves on the road on the premise that because they can move the vehicle, they can drive, until the unexpected happens.

It may take a longer time, but don't break the rules. It may appear like everyone has left you behind, but still don't break the rules. If you're patient with a consistent disciplined pattern, you will reap the benefits of your actions. Don't jump the gun if you don't want to be disqualified.

The need for common sense: as you go on the direction to your destination, there is the need for common sense. If you don't have one, you will be misdirected. For instance, when you're looking for a direction, asking certain people for help is a waste of time because they will add to your confusion for one or more reasons. Some people lack the vocabulary of description; instead of telling you to go right, they will direct you to the left. For some, they may not know the direction, but still tell you to go somewhere. And for others, they don't know at all where you're going. So, common sense is necessary to know when someone is misdirecting you; it is also necessary, to help you grasp the description when being told the right direction. Some people have gone the wrong way because they didn't have enough sense to know that someone was misleading them. Common sense isn't a course in the University; it is a lifetime course. You learn it from the seat of wisdom and certain life experiences.

DESTINATION

A student that gains admission into the university has one destination in mind; to obtain a degree. A couple that just married has one destination in mind; to forever live happily together. Everyone with purpose has a destination; to end successfully. That successful destination is the picture everyone must paint in the mind. Without that picture, you will walk pass your future unnoticed; structured mental picture prevents you from walking pass your future unnoticed. Rather than paint structured mental pictures, some people paint confusion, and also end up confused. The picture you paint is determined by your decision; decisions either vote for life or death. Some life isn't instant; it takes a painstaking process. Some death isn't also instant; the consequence of a bad decision may take ages before manifesting. Your final home is a consequence of your final decision. Your final home is your destination.

Destinations go beyond secular official positions. Happiness is destination. Peace is destination. Good relationship is destination. So, you may make all the money on earth; occupy all the top positions; if it doesn't make you truly have that inner joy and peace, you have missed your destiny.

Where is destination?

Destination is a place of assignment: a place of assignment is a place of responsibilities. You are not on top to topple people; you are there to serve people. Some people think that they're up there to be served; they don't realise that they're there to wash the feet of the disciples. So, when the led stretch their feet to be washed, they smack their legs, and tell them how dirty and smelly their feet are. If you can't wash stinking feet, you're not a leader. It is your responsibility to clean them up and perfume them until they glow to the world. If you've never made the forsaken and despondent glow, you haven't done your job yet.

Destination is a place of taking responsibilities: performing your assignment and taking responsibilities are two different things. Some people perform their tasks excellently well, but when things go wrong, they absolve themselves of any blame. If you lead, the errors of the led are entirely yours, even if you may not be directly responsible. Every purposeful destination is a place of taking responsibilities. If you don't like taking responsibilities, remain where you are. Unfortunately, those who fear success actually remain where they are. There is the story of a man with postgraduate degree and professional qualifications in his field that chose to be a bus driver because of the fear of taking responsibilities. He says drivers are dumb, and if they make errors, management will understand. But I know lots of highly intelligent drivers with fantastic leadership skills. I guess, he's the one that is dumb!

Destination is a place on the mountain top: on the mountain top, you can't hide; you are exposed. Everything you do on top is in public glare, so, beware. The light from the sky exposes you first, before reaching those at the foot of the mountain. If there's promotion, you get it first; if there's demotion, you also get it first. You're the first to design, and the first to resign, if you're truly a responsible leader. You're on the frontline when the enemy calls and on the backline when they're chasing. You die first, but also quickly resurrect first in order to give life to those you lead. You're on the mountain top, not to show off, but to protect and provide for those whose staircase you climbed to get there.

Destination is a place of temptation: when on top, you're always tempted to look down. When you do, you feel dizzy; down-looking people are dizzy people; never look down, except you want to help those that are down to the top.

There are Chief Executive Officers that look down; they end up sleeping with their Personal Assistants. There are sportsmen that look down; they end up taking performance enhancing drugs. There are governments and leaders that look down; they end up embezzling public funds. Destination is a place of temptation; if you don't resist it, you will fall.

Destination is a place of attraction and distraction. Both take you off track. Attraction is seductive; distraction is deductive. Seduction and deduction are anti-goal realisation; with them, you need no other enemy of vision. Seduction and deduction never paid the price; they're not on top to win; they're already losers waiting to bring down people's aspirations. If you don't understand their game, you will play with them, and they'll beat you silly, and put you in a state of ridicule. If you do understand, you'll either beat them or avoid them. My advice is; avoid them!

Destination is a place of legacy: in every destination, there's an entry stage and exit stage; you won't occupy forever. As you exit, there's always something you leave behind. It is called legacy. Legacy is what will keep recalling your presence even when you're gone; it is either positive or negative. Great vision plan put in place that continues growing an organisation you're no longer heading is a positive legacy. Wrong strategic policies that make the organisation stagnant are also a legacy, but a bad one. Your legacies live after you; they never die with you. That is why you must be careful what you do. At destination, you're already a leader, so, lead with caution.

Destination is a place of retirement: one way or the other, a man's time will be up, either by definition or by death whether he likes it or not. You won't be there forever, so have a succession plan. Succession plan must begin immediately you sit on your throne. Don't wait until your exit stage to start getting ready someone that will lead the next phase of the vision. Begin immediately; begin now. It takes a lifetime to raise a successor. Some successors don't have wisdom, so, you must keep preaching until they start comprehending. Some successors believe that you got to where you are by presenting nice speeches; they need to be taught how to die first, before living. As you think retirement, think succession. What will life be after you're gone? Can the future hope on you for beauty or for beast? Your actions today, are the only ones that can answer those questions!

CHAPTER SEVEN

5 THINGS YOU MUST NOT LOSE AS A VISIONARY

One major attribute of icons is their ability to be visionary. All the icons the world has produced have the ability to behold the future and make meaning out of it. Many of them were able to tackle their humble beginnings because they could see better tomorrows. You too can be an icon because even with your eyes closed, you can imagine things on your mind, and if you can, it means you also have the innate ability to be creative. Creativity does not only mean being able to make things with your hands or design some extraordinary software; your little suggestion in a team meeting can turn to be something that will change the world. Don't hold back your positive inner thoughts; they may form the new invention that the world requires to step out of economic crunch. Don't think that you're insignificant; don't believe that the best brains have said it all, or done it all; as unique as you are, so are your ideas; paint the ideas on the wall, don't be ashamed to air your opinion. The world needs you because you are an unpublished icon.

Who is a visionary?

1. A visionary is a person that turns an impractical, not presently workable idea into reality. That idea you consider to be crazy may be what will change your life. The idea to set up the social

media was crazy to an ordinary mind; he could not imagine why billions of people all over the world would agree to connect on a single platform. In his mind, he never believed that one day, people can send messages to each other and instantly, the recipient gets the mail. But today, the impossibility has become a reality. Your idea can become real even if those around you refuse to believe you. If everyone believes you, whatever you're doing is common; people easily believe common things. If your idea is beyond many people's imaginations, then, it is worth fighting for. What makes you visionary is because the picture painted on your mind is unique to you. Many may think you're insane for ever creating that imagination, but do you know what, big dreams have always, and will continue to be insane!

2. A visionary is a person that transforms an imagination into an outward manifestation. A transform is a creative change. Don't let your positive imagination die within you; transform it into what everyone can see. Until is becomes visible, you can't win converts. No one signed up on Facebook until in 2004 when it became visible. No one used the internet until it became visible. No one read this book until it became visible. If I had left it at the level of my mind, who would go into my mind to read the unseen prints? You need to push your dream outward for the world to see. Icon-ism is defined by visible actions; don't die a dreamer; die a transformer.

3. A visionary is a person with an unusually keen foresight. Keenness is sharpness, strength and distinctiveness of perception. Perception is the ability to see and comprehend what common minds cannot understand. You are not a common mind; you were created to be a think tank. In you are loads of information ready for download; the only difference is that you haven't realised it. Until you do, you will continue to believe in the impossible. Get up and say to yourself, 'I'm a visionary, I have foresight. I can perceive. I am sharp and intelligent.'

4. A visionary is a dreamer. A dreamer is a person with successive creative imaginations in the inner recesses of his heart. Successive creative imagination is a continuous thread or sequence of uninterrupted flow of ideas being turned into action. You may begin with one idea, but as you work on that one, more will follow. Any assignment you accomplish has a unique way of introducing new and better assignments. So, work on what you have now, so that what you have now will bring to you, what you don't have. If you understand this principle, you'll come to know that responsibilities grow through accomplishment. As you act on one, you mature into dealing with more.

5. A visionary is a talented and gifted entrepreneur with winning mentality, willing and ready to positively affect the world. You are talented; yes, you are. I don't like it, when some people think that they're being humble when they say that they aren't talented. Where did they get their definitions of talent from? One way or the other, everyone is talented. Talent is diverse; for the fact you aren't in what is perceived to be mega talent does not mean that you aren't. For example, everyone can't sing, no matter how you train some people's voices, they will still croak like a frog. For the fact they can't sing does not mean that they aren't talented; they are definitely talented in other areas that may not be needed on the stage. Listen; everyone isn't cut out for the stage. Some people's talents are at the back of the stage, but without them, there wouldn't be a stage. If you are on stage, respect those at the back of the stage if you really want to continue being there because if they pull the plug on you, your microphone will stop working!

5 things you must not lose as a visionary

1. Don't lose your fire: every visionary has a fire. The fire is what keeps him going. The fire is what cooks the meal of the vision until it is ready to be served. Without the fire, a visionary cannot be on fire. Without the fire, there can't be a drive. Without the fire, there is no motion. If a car must accelerate, it must be on

fire. If a ship must sail, it must be on fire. If an aeroplane must fly, it must be on fire. If a vision must actualise, it must be on fire. Without the fire, there won't be a fulfilment.

What is this fire?

a. Your fire is your enthusiasm for the vision: Your enthusiasm is your undying interest. The enthusiasm for the vision must possess your mind. If it doesn't, it means you've lost your fire. If you call it a vision but lack undying interest in and for it, you have no fire. If you lose the fire for the vision, there's no way it is going to manifest.

b. Your fire is your excitement for the vision: every man that births a vision must be excited about the vision. A vision is a baby; if you're not excited about it, you have no right to be excited when you birth a human baby, because without a vision, any human baby you birth doesn't have a future.

c. Your fire is your liveliness: liveliness is spark, activity and being vigorous. You can't be on fire and not produce a spark. Your spark is your charge. Without a charge, a battery cannot function. Without a functioning battery, your car or mobile phone cannot work. If your car or mobile phone doesn't work, you will lose your mobility or ability to communicate as you wish. Liveliness is fire; don't lose it.

d. Your fire is your eagerness, intensity, zeal and zest: eagerness is being earnest and having a longing for something. You must have a longing for your vision if you truly love your vision. You must be earnest about your vision if you really desire it. If you're not eager about your vision, it means you've lost your fire. Don't lose your fire for fulfilling that calling. Keep your flame because it will soon be fame.

e. Your fire is your explosion: an explosion is a blast. Let your vision be a blast. An explosion causes a bursting noise. Make noise about your vision if you truly believe in it. An explosion is a sudden, rapid or great increase. Make sure your vision expands; don't leave it in a stationary and stagnant position. A man that is on fire does not make his vision idle.

f. Your fire is your passion and inspiration: passion is a powerful and compelling love for something. Inspiration is the power of influence. As a visionary, you must not lose your passion and inspiration. Any visionary that loses these two powerful tools has actually lost his vision. No passion, no vision. No inspiration, no vision.

2. Don't lose your hunger: without hunger, you cannot eat; without eating, you cannot grow. If you stop growing, you start depreciating. After a while, you start dying in bits until you're finally gone. A visionary that is satisfied, gradually kills the vision. The one that is ever hungry feeds the vision, therefore, it continues to grow and live. A growing and living vision is the one that stands out and takes the centre stage.

What is hunger?

a. Hunger is anger: it is often said that a hungry man is an angry man; that is true. If you're not angry with where your vision currently is, you can't move it forward. The easiest way to identify visionaries who have lost their hunger is by looking at their anger. If they feel cool where they are, they will remain where they are. Positive irritation is a key to progression. Positive anger is the channel through which positive changes occur. Never lose your anger if you want to manifest the best in your vision.

b. Hunger is yearning, craving and desire: yearning is a type of attraction towards something. Yearning is a feeling of affection for a thing. A crave is an eager desire for something, while desire is a longing or craving for something that brings satisfaction or enjoyment.

Everyday, you must yearn, crave and desire for the fulfilment of your vision. You mustn't lose that hunger. Any vision that you don't crave for will not make way for you. Any vision that you don't yearn for, you can't earn from. Any vision that you do not desire will easily expire. So, don't lose your yearn, crave and desire because these form part of your hunger.

c. **Hunger is an urge:** an urge is a push, press or force towards a target. An urge also means to impel, constrain, or move in taking certain actions in a certain direction. Your vision must impel you to move in a purposeful direction. If it doesn't, it means you've lost your hunger. Your vision must be a driving force of change. Your vision must be a motivation for you to push and press towards that mark of success. Your vision must be an advancing force that will propel you towards that target that you've set for yourself. So, don't lose your urge. If you lose your urge, you will lose your hunger. If you lose your hunger, you will lose the entire vision. Be hungry; always be hungry. If you're full, quickly digest what you've eaten so that you can starve again. There are lots of food that will keep growing that vision, except you're hungry, you can't eat it.

d. **Hunger is willingness:** willingness is being disposed towards something. It is a cheerful readiness or consent to do something. Another attribute of hunger is willingness. If you're not willing, you're not hungry. You must be willing to continue pursuing your vision until it becomes manifest. Your will makes a way for your vision. It doesn't just make a way but also creates the wheel to drive the vision. Never lose your willingness to keep going until you reach the place you see in the inner recesses of your heart. Never lose your hunger; never lose your willingness.

e. **Hunger is aspiration:** aspiration is a goal, objective or aim. Aspiration is something ahead of you. A visionary must always have something ahead of him. If there's nothing ahead of you,

you're either heading nowhere or simply straying. Stagnancy and stray are relatives standing on a keg of gun powder. Disaster locates an idle person while the stray locates disaster. Either way, both relatives are subject to danger. Anyone immersed in positive aspiration always locates a positive destination. Don't lose your aspiration; don't lose your hunger.

d. Hunger is related to thirst: hunger and thirst are related because they both involve ingestion of food whether solid or liquid. I have never seen a hungry man that does not thirst. I have never seen a man who eats food without drinking one form of liquid or the other. No matter how much food you eat, if you don't take a drink, you will die of dehydration.

A visionary that does not thirst will dehydrate. Thirst makes you go for liquid. Liquid softens your solid, and makes it easily digestible. If your solid does not digest, what should make you grow will end up causing you unusual pain. Certain strategic information and decisions are solid. They need excellent communication which is the liquid to pass the message to subordinates. If you pass some information down the chain raw, you will be sending a wrong message. A wrong message triggers a cascade of negative reactions.

Visionaries who don't thirst kill the taste of the food that was meant to activate growth. Never lose your thirst; never lose your hunger.

3. Don't lose your oil: 'What has oil got to do with being a visionary?' Someone may ask. The 'oil' is just being used metaphorically, as it represents some vital attributes that a visionary must not lose in order to excel in the fulfilment of his vision.

What does oil signify?

a. Oil is a symbol of lubrication: where there is no lubrication, there will be negative friction. Negative friction results in unnecessary heat; unnecessary heat results in unnecessary tension. A visionary should constantly have that attitude of easing tensions between two or more joints that are connected. Challenges will always emerge when pursuing a vision, but the manner and approach of dealing with such challenges are determinants of the visionary's ability to manage change or differences. There can't be smooth movement of a vision from stage to stage when two bones that should fuse peacefully together are knocking each other. Therefore, a visionary must not lose his oil, otherwise; he will lose his lubrication.

b. Oil is a symbol of energy: energy is defined as the capacity to do work. Capacity is the maximum amount of a substance that a container can obtain. So, the size of a container is the capacity of the container. A visionary must not lose his energy, otherwise; he will lose his capacity. If he loses his capacity, he loses his size; if he loses his size, he loses his status. What a visionary should do is to continue increasing his energy so that he can achieve more.

c. Oil is a symbol of ability: ability is power, competence, intelligence, proficiency, capability and comprehension. No visionary should dare lose any of these attributes. Nothing meaningful can be achieved without any of these things. Strive to maintain or better still, increase your oil. Don't run out; don't dry out. Always reorder these oils when they're going down because without them, you can't achieve anything purposeful and meaningful.

4. Don't lose your wine: for a liquid to be called wine, it must have been in form of sugar fermented by yeast to convert it to alcohol. Every vision begins with ideas. Typically, any idea that is born is sweet; so to say. A new idea is like sugar to the tongue, but for it to manifest, it must go from sweetness to 'wine-ness'. As it is clearly known, wine makes you tipsy. Tipsiness is intoxication. Do you realise that if your vision does not intoxicate you, it cannot take you anywhere? There are lots of people that were initially intoxicated by their visions, but when they encountered some roadblocks, lost their intoxications, therefore, they lost the drive to fulfil the visions. You can't be excited by what does not intoxicate you. You can't bring down the barriers that are limiting a vision that you're not drunk with. It is intoxication that will make you push beyond the status quo. It is intoxication that will make you run the distance at unimaginable speed. It is intoxication that will make you jump the fence that separates you from reaching the ultimate goal of your vision. If you lose your wine, you can't be intoxicated. Intoxication gives you the elation, buzz, charge, delight, joy and rapture. Never lose your wine, because if you do, your vision will be dead before it ever germinates.

5. Don't lose your mind: losing the mind doesn't necessary mean going crazy. Inability to properly manage pressures makes you lose your mind. If you cannot prioritise, you will lose your mind. If you don't use the principle of scale of preference, you will lose your mind. A loss of mind is a loss of focus, attention, concentration and sense of reasoning. When your focus is broken due to one thing or the other, your attention will be divided. With a divided attention, you can't adequately deal with issues that are vision related. Vision related issues require one hundred percent focus and attention.

CHAPTER EIGHT

HOW TO SET AND SCORE LIFETIME GOALS

An icon stands out. What makes him stand out is the ability to set and score goals. Without goals, no one can win. It is goals that make a person or a team to be ahead. Icons are goal scorers. A goal is a target that everyone wants to reach. The weak wants to reach it; the strong also wants to. The reason everyone wants to score goals is because goals define victory; goals define who a winner or champion is. The more you outscore an opponent, the more you move towards being crowned a champion. Without goals, there will be no gold. To reach that place where you can be celebrated, you must score and continue to score until the game is over. Sleeping during the game on the premise that you're leading can spell doom, because your opponent can take advantage of your slip to slam you with a heavy defeat.

What is a goal?

- **A goal is a destination:** destination is a purpose, intention, aim, objective or target. It is the place a person wants to get to. Every icon has a destination he wants to reach. That destination is boldly painted as a picture in his mind. He sees that picture daily and gradually but consistently runs towards that picture in order to cross the finish line. That picture inspires him in spite of the obstacles all around him. Whenever he wants to give up, he keeps seeing the destination of his true expectation; his goal. His goals are his driving force. His goals are his motivation to keep beating the odds. His goals make him accelerate towards a place of achievement.

- **A goal is an expected result or achievement towards which effort is directed:** efforts without results are a waste of useful energy. The desire of every icon is to produce expected results. The goal of a basketball player is to keep putting the ball into the net. The goal of a boxer is to keep punching the face of his opponent. It won't be an expected result for a basketball player to make all the efforts of taking the ball to the net but dropping it outside the net. You don't win by dropping your ball outside the net. It is also a waste of strength and time for a boxer to keep hitting his opponent on the tummy without targeting his face. Points aren't scored hitting tummies.

- **A goal is a vision where a man concentrates his focus and attention with determination in order to obtain an outstanding result:** focus and attention are major tools required to achieve success in every endeavour of life. Without these tools, no goal can be attained. The people that succeeded made it because they were focused. Showing full concentration on your vision and calling with unqualified determination is what makes you an icon. If you want to rule in your pursuit, you can only achieve it with your heart, mind and body fully focused on what you do. Your focus will be tested by different forms of distractions, but your resolve to keep going in spite of the obvious barriers ahead of you, and the backstabbers behind you, or the wagging tongues of spectators beside you, or maybe, the competitors running against you is what will determine your success or failure. If your eyes are on your goal, you cannot fail.

- **A goal is the terminal end of a race or a place where points are scored:** for a 100m runner, the goal is to be the first to cross that finish line. If at the end of that race, nothing is won, crossing the finish line means nothing because nothing is achieved. To make an impression on the minds of people, cross that line with success. Anything short of victory wasn't made for you; you were born to win. If you are desirous, you can win. The icons of yesterday or today didn't stop at the doorstep of success; they entered into it. They didn't find it easier than you; on most cases, it was even more difficult for them, but the hunger to become winners kept them on the pedestrian of determination until they emerged. They didn't stop trying in spite of their frequent failures; the more they failed, the more they tried because they believed in their hearts that one day, they'll win. Because of this undying belief, they ended up winning. You too can win, where everyone said it was impossible. You can prove to the world that you're not just on earth to compete, you are here to win!

What are the factors that define your goals?

- **Your purpose must define your goals:** purpose is the reason for which something exists. I am of a very strong opinion that everyone was born for a purpose; no one is useless. I am also of a very strong opinion that everyone was born not just for a purpose but for a specific purpose. If a man was born for a specific purpose, it is expedient for him, before leaving this earth to fulfil his reason for being born. If he doesn't, his time on earth was wasted doing something he wasn't born for. I believe that for a man to set meaningful goals, he must first understand why he's on earth. If he does, he can then set goals in line with his purpose. Any major goal set outside purpose is an abuse of goal setting. Many people have set goals based on intellectual understanding, without realising that purpose is stronger than intelligence. In spite of a lot of

139

people setting what is perceived to be fantastic goals, they end up with inner dissatisfaction after achieving those goals. The reason for this inner dissatisfaction is because something called purpose is missing. Without purpose, goals can be misleading. To set a purposeful goal, discover your purpose!

- **Your need defines your goals:** The word 'Goal' is very broad because there are different types of goals depending on the person involved. What a goal is to one person may not be what it is to another. To a person, getting to the highest position in his career may be his goal while to another, living healthily may be his. Therefore, people set goals based on their needs rather than their wants. To some people, setting financial goals may be their priorities; to others, it could be educational, relationship, family or business goals. Whatever it is, your need must define your goals. If you don't need it, don't set it. What is the need of a Geography Professor setting a goal to run a Bachelor's degree programme in Geography? It doesn't make sense because he doesn't need it. But the unfortunate thing is that there are people ignorantly duplicating what they have already achieved in the name of goals.

- **Your skills define your goals:** this may not be applicable to everyone, but there are certain goals that do require skills. If you're not skilled in it, don't set it. For example, if an accountant sets a goal of finishing a company's balance sheet in two weeks, it will be silly for someone who doesn't have any knowledge of accounting to set the same goal. If a medical doctor sets a goal of attending to fifty patients in the next one month, it will be absurd for a teacher to set the same goal because for him to achieve it, it may take ages. So, your skill must define your goal.

- **Your expectation defines your goals:** we all have expectations; people also have certain expectations from/of us. Many times, I hear some people say, 'Don't compare me with anyone. We all have our lives to live'. These people may be right in some ways, but not always because, there are certain goals you expect people on the same level to achieve. If one person is not pulling his weight, he will definitely be compared to someone on his level because they were offered the same level of privileges under the same conditions. For example, two students in the same class under the same conditions are expected to perform well. If one, in spite of all the resources is lagging behind, the basis for comparison comes in. So, a student who understands his expectations will set a goal to achieve excellence in his examinations. His expectation of excellence will become his driving force for hard work. Expectation, therefore, is a factor that defines the setting of a goal.

- **Your beliefs define your goals; your beliefs define your mindset:** What you believe prompts you to set certain goals. If you have a champion's mindset, you will always set goals that will help you maintain your status as a champion. The world champions that have continuously stood out developed the mindset that they will continue to be champions; therefore, they kept setting goals that will stretch them in order to maintain their positions. If on the contrary, they had the belief of win some, lose some, their performances will also undulate. Your belief system strongly influences your goal setting.

- **Your failures define your goals:** when I was a student, I wasn't always performing excellently well. I had no one to mentor me; the only educational mentor I had was failure. Not that I actually failed, but sometimes, I wasn't satisfied with my performances. Anytime I performed below my expectation, I considered it a failure. I was always angry with failure; this anger always woke me up from sleep so that I can work hard. The results that accompanied my failures were outstanding. Anytime I failed, I would set very high goals of becoming one of the best in the class; and I always did. Failure can positively define your goal setting if you know how to manage it. But the pitfall for some people is that when they fail, rather than use it as a motivation, they get demotivated and lower their goals. I do realise that setting immeasurable and unachievable goals is senseless, but if the goal is measurable and achievable, failure should charge you up to succeed rather than put you in a state of indifference or despondency.

- **Your association defines your goal setting:** your relationship affects your goal setting. Peer pressure is one major factor that either improves or disapproves your goal setting. You can't achieve less or better than the people you always hang out with. There is a high tendency that birds of the same feathers flock together. From various social and psychology researches, it is a proven fact that relationship determines status. If you work in an environment where everyone is driving for excellence, if you do not follow suite, you will feel odd; so, you have no alternative but to do what everyone is doing. If you also work in an environment where there is no drive, any goal you set above your peers, you will consider high because you're like one eyed man in the city of the blind. The goal you've set may be ordinary in a purpose driven environment but because you're somewhere with little or no motivation to set good goals, you'll feel like a star. Your association definitely defines your goal setting.

How to set and score goals

I usually say that goal setting is great, but it is possible to set goals and not score goals. The one who scores is the one who wins; therefore, the major challenge with winning is the ability to score. So many people have set goals but never scored goals; as a result, the difference they were intending to make did not manifest. It takes a lot to set goals; it even takes more to score.

To understand goal setting and scoring, using a football game as illustration is a perfect example. I will therefore, use it as my basis of explanation as I deal with the following points.

- **To set and score lifetime goals, you must walk in your area of talent:** anyone who wants to become a professional footballer must first of all be talented in playing football. Sometimes, I see some parents take their children weekly to practice football for the purpose of embracing it as a career. As I take a closer look, it becomes more obvious that most of these children are not gifted in playing football; but because of the fame and money involved in it, some parents' sense of reasoning become blinded until it is sometimes too late for the child. If a child is forced to set a goal in an area that isn't his, he may never score. If he doesn't score, he may never win. So, the first thing a man must realise is that he must set a lifetime goal in his gifting. Its needless pursuing a career or vision that is unrelated to your destiny. Put your time, energy and other life building resources in your area of talent; put it in your calling. If you put your resources in your calling, one day, people who matter will start calling you; but if you don't, those that will call you will be those that have also missed their ways.

- **To set and score lifetime goals, you must add skills to your gift:** a gift is not a skill; it is only a potential; it is only a talent. Just like every talent, a gift is a special natural ability or aptitude. Talent alone doesn't do it; it is the building of your ability that makes you skilful. Whether you accept it or not, I believe that I'm a gifted writer, but when I started, I wasn't skilful because I made serious punctuation blunders. In order to take my gift to a higher level, I began developing the skills of writing; I started learning the skills of punctuations, proofreading, copy editing, etc. By doing that, my writing gift began to improve. In the same vein, a talented footballer must acquire the skills of the game before being considered a professional. There are many gifted footballers that fell from grace to grass because they ignored the wisdom of continually updating their skills; they felt talent alone could do it, but it never did. What makes you skilful are practice, updates and research.

- **To set and score lifetime goals, you must always prepare:** a footballer cannot set and score goals without proper preparation. The skills exhibited on the pitch did not start from the pitch; it started behind the pitch. The training never took place during the match; it took place during the mask. No one saw the man in the mask; no one saw the wears and tears undergone by the man who was daily preparing in the dark. Becoming the highest goal scorer does not come from playing football on a computer game; it comes from rigorous hardwork behind the scene. Therefore, prepare if you really want to score lifetime goals.

- **To set and score lifetime goals, be a team player:** no matter how gifted a person may be in playing football, if he doesn't join a team, his dream of setting and scoring goals will be defeated. You need a team to be a winner. You need a team to be a champion. You need a team to be on top. Without a team, there will be no theme. Even in one man sports, there are teams. The members of the team are all involved in making sure that that one man wins the game. You can't set and score goals without a team. A tennis professional has his team. A boxer has his team. An entrepreneur has his team. When you're in a team, realise that victory does not belong to you alone. You're not the only one involved in the team; therefore, it shouldn't be all about you. Have a team; be a team player.

- **To set and score lifetime goals, practice with your teammates:** I have heard of fantastic footballers that either dodge training or arrogantly refuse to train with their teammates because they feel that they're better. Not too long, you also hear the sad news of their retrogressions. Pride and arrogance kill lifetime goals. Even if you're the best in your team, practice with your teammates; if you don't, you will fade away. Fading away means unfulfilled dreams. During practice, strategies are devised; during practice, opponents and potential opponents or competitors' strengths and weaknesses are analysed. During practice, game plans are discussed and conclusions made. How can you determine what the game plan is, if you don't practice with teammates? You can't set and score valuable goals when you refuse to practice with teammates!

- **To set and score lifetime goals, always be determined to make the first team:** those who make the first team always play in valuable matches; not just friendlies. Don't die a substitute; be determined to be in the main event. Making the first team gives you the privilege to set and score goals; no one on the bench can score goals because it is against the rule to have a twelfth man on the pitch. You can't score from the bench; be determined to be in the game. Being in the game means you're one of the best. If your team can do without you, it means you're not adding much value to them.

- **To set and score lifetime goals, follow the game plan:** every game has a game plan. No professional coach would send his team into a game without a plan. The plan is the approach that the coach deems fit for the game after doing a competitor analysis. Every disciplined player would follow a game plan; that is what makes him a professional. In spite of game plans, some players follow their own mediocre plans and

145

end up messing up the game. Some teams lose, not because they didn't prepare well but because someone felt he knew more than the coach and decided to do his own thing. Doing your own thing, most times, is detrimental especially when you're going against some set rules or standards.

- **To set and score lifetime goals, you must be flexible:** no matter how excellent a game plan may be, it doesn't always work because the strength and tactics of your opponent determine your ability to set and score goals. If the tactics isn't working, be ready for a change; don't be rigid. Rigidity is lack of flexibility; rigidity means that the person isn't versatile. Everyone who wants to set and score goals must be ready to adapt to new changes in rules and regulations, even if it has to be sudden. Always be ready for change; that is the attitude of a professional.

- **To set and score lifetime goals, you must be ready to follow the rules of the game:** every game has rules; they are the dos and don'ts; they are the laws of the game. It is the rules that draw the line of discipline. Just like in every typical institution, there is someone or some people assigned to enforce the laws. In the case of football, it is the referee. If you're determined to set and score lifetime goals, there must be a referee to instil discipline. If your goals have no referee, no matter how many times you score, it will amount to nothing. Every goal scored must have a governing body responsible for managing and regulating how things are done. If you play alone, score alone, regulate yourself all alone, compete with yourself alone, win alone and award trophies to yourself alone; you are revolving in self deception. Every meaningful goal you set and score has management bodies behind it; they may not be formal bodies, but behind the scene, there are people who ensure that you don't play waywardly. If you refuse to deliberately put yourself under lifetime goal's regulatory bodies, life itself will regulate you by teaching you a serious lesson.

- **To set and score lifetime goals, don't play to the gallery:** children entertain spectators; adults score goals. To be a winner, you don't need entertainment; what you need are the goals. To score goals, your attention must not be on the spectators. Your fans may want you to shoot when it's not convenient or result oriented; don't shoot because you want to please them; only shoot when it will yield the right result. The opponent's fans may rain insults and abuses on you; don't focus on them. You aren't there to play against their fans; you are there to play against the opposing men on the pitch. Never play to the gallery; playing to the gallery makes you lose focus. When your focus is gone, your game is gone.

- **To set and score lifetime goals, you need to have stamina:** sometimes, life is an opponent rather than a friend; so, it will stretch you until you prove that you have the stamina to withstand it and win. Not all games end within the regulation time; some require extra time especially if a winner must emerge. If you don't have the stamina, you can't set and score lifetime goals. Whether you are the one that set them or someone else, the truth is that great goals stretch. For anything that stretches, you need the stamina to withstand and overcome it.

- **To set and score lifetime goals, you must have the ability to soak pressure:** stamina deals more with physical strength or fatigue, but pressure focuses on the mind. Man's greatest strength comes from his ability to appropriately use his mind. When you set goals, all forms of pressures target your mind. There are two forms of pressures; the internal and external. Internal pressures come from within; external pressures come from outside. The fear of losing is an internal pressure. The fear of not scoring is also an internal pressure. Some external pressures can come from your own team; your coach, manager, teammates, fans, etc. Some external pressures can also come

147

from the opposing team or spectators. Wherever it comes from, to set and score goals, you must have the ability to soak pressures. The ability to soak pressure is a great attribute in leadership. If you cannot soak pressure, you cannot score. If you cannot soak pressure, even if you score, you may end up conceding more than you've scored.

- **To set and score lifetime goals, you must be focused:** focus requires all your attention in looking, beholding or seeing just one thing; no one can score without focus. Your physical eyes don't need to see it before focusing on it. The best form of focus is mental focus. I have seen a few professional footballers score tremendous goals without facing the goal post. In spite of the fact that they weren't physically looking at the goal posts, their mental eyes were. A mental focus is all you need to set and score lifetime goals. No matter how spiritual you are, if you're not mentally focused, you can't win.

- **To set and score lifetime goals, you must have a winning mindset:** a mindset is a mental perception, i.e. the way a person sees things. A person's perception determines his actions, and his actions determine his outcome. If a person believes that he's a failure, no amount of money can make him successful. If a person also believes that he's a success, no amount of intimidation can stop him from being successful. Your mindset either helps you score or miss. When a footballer wants to take a penalty kick, from the look on his face, you can sometimes determine if he will score or miss because mindset never hides its identity. So, to set or score lifetime goals, be determined to have a winning mindset.

- **To set and score lifetime goals, hit your target:** in most matches, many footballers set up goals but never score goals. To score goals, you must hit your target. As you hit the target, remember that there is a goalkeeper who is there to stop you. So, as you hit the ball, place it at an angle that the goalkeeper cannot reach. Every goal cannot be scored by hitting it hard; sometimes, you need to be subtle in order to score. Don't always approach your target like a bully; sometimes, be tricky.

As I conclude on this, realise that even if it's a one man game, lifetime goals are set and scored by a team. If you know how to network and manage healthy relationships, you can't hit amiss. Go ahead and score; its all yours for the taking and the winning!

CHAPTER NINE

HOW TO GENERATE IDEAS AND DEVELOP THEM

Idea generation and development are principal actions that icons take in order to come up with winning formulas. When they find the right formula, they stick to it until positive results begin to emanate. One basic thing icons understand is that a good formula may not bring automatic results, so, they are ready to wait and push until they get their expectations.

Without fresh ideas, new things don't happen. What makes you always new is because of the new information that you generate one way or the other. If you want your business, talent, or any of your pursuits to gain fresh attention, the need for idea generation and development cannot be overemphasised.

When it comes to idea generation, many people are lost because their heads can only think of a few things, or maybe, just one thing, or sometimes, nothing. What kills an endeavour is when visionaries continue to follow only one approach. Different people see differently, so, using different pictures to communicate a message will help you reach more people. There are big companies that have folded up; there are also certain highly talented people that their reigns were abruptly cut short because they couldn't innovate. Innovation is essential for renovation.

The need to talk about how ideas are generated will help people think outside the box. The methods of idea generation are definitely not confined to the suggestions I have offered in this chapter, but they are enough approaches to help a person that is in need of coming up with some purposeful information in his or her assignment.

What is an idea?

1. An idea is a conception: conception is the origin or beginning of a thing. Conception is inception of pregnancy. For a woman to give birth, she must conceive and for her to conceive, that idea called sperm and ovum must come together to produce the zygote; zygote is a fertilised egg. This zygote grows in the womb of the woman until the due date. The baby that is born began as an idea. At inception, it may have looked insignificant, but the big man that is the President or Prime Minister of your country was that little unnoticed thing. The Chief Executive Officers of the topmost organisations were first ideas conceived in the wombs of their mums before they were born. The big companies they manage were also conceptions before they were developed to the level they are today. Don't feel small when you conceive an idea; look at the destination of that idea, not the situation. It is the ability to look at the destination that makes you a visionary. Again, don't allow anyone insult your pregnancy; don't allow anyone talk down on your so called little idea. It may be little now, but when you work on it, no one will have the audacity to walk on it.

2. An idea is a thought: a thought is the act, process, capacity or faculty of thinking. Every idea begins with a thought; without that, you can't create. Ruminating on a productive idea makes it a dream. The more you ponder on it, the more you see the bigger picture. No one else may see that picture except you; no one else may understand the roadmap you're beholding except you. Since you alone may be the one seeing vividly your destination, don't be offended or abandon your dream because someone else can't envision where you're going. Some people may even have the capacity to see your destination but out of envy, may decide to ridicule your dream so as to discourage you from carrying on. The outward manifestation of your thoughts is entirely dependent on your determination to ignore dissidents from infiltrating your dream. Promote your thoughtful ideas; work on them. Don't abandon your dream.

3. An idea is a notion: a notion is an ingenious idea or device. An ingenious idea is an idea that is characterised by cleverness or originality of invention or construction. An ingenious idea is resourceful. Sometimes, these ingenious ideas appear vague, but may end up becoming outstanding. Great ideas sometimes don't appear like they are, until the results begin to surface. It wasn't a great idea for man to go into the bottom of the sea to drill petroleum; it was unimaginable until some great minds defied the fear of the waters and dared the huge waves. They made it happen. Today, we have offshore oil benefits; a product of human imagination.

4. An idea is an impression: an impression is a strong effect, mark, indentation or figure produced by pressure. For an impression to be imprinted there must be pressure; every pressure requires a force. That pressure is what makes the signs on a stamp to stick on a paper. The signs from a stamp on papers are seals of endorsement. If you want to endorse your destiny or make other people endorse you, produce a killer idea that is unique to your calling. A killer idea makes impressions. IPad was a killer idea; it has made an indelible impression. The social media was a killer idea; it is an incurable virus that the whole world cannot do without. Make an impression; come up with your idea. There's something in there that you haven't taken advantage of. You think you don't have it, but you actually do!

5. An idea is a view and opinion: to have a view, you must have good eyesight. Eyesight is not just physical, it is also mental. A blind mind cannot generate good ideas. Apart from mental sight, a view is a representation of a person, group or organisation. Your view is your input into a general opinion. Opinion is a judgment, belief, evaluation, assessment, appraisal, presumption, hypothesis or supposition.

Don't ever suppress your opinion because you don't know how helpful or useful it may be. Don't ever hide your views because it may be the creative idea that is required to bring the change that is most needed. Out of self esteem issues, some people erroneously assume that no good idea can come out of them, and as a result, they always keep quiet when topics of relevant subjects are discussed. Listen; it isn't a man's level of education or qualification that determines his ability to come up with super ideas; it is a thing of perception. So, don't keep silent when you should be speaking. It will be nice if you can emulate someone I know. Her grammatical expressions are unpardonably flawed, but one thing she has working for her is her personality; no one can stop her from talking in spite of her poor spoken English. In short, she may even be the one to raise a discussion among original blue eye English people. For that attribute of self confidence, I highly admire her!

6. An idea is an intention: intention is design, purpose, aim, motive or determination. Anything that is an intention is also a goal. Nothing great is created without a great goal. Your goal determines your role.

An intention isn't just your motive as an individual; it also involves your reason for being on earth. You were an intention created to achieve a certain purpose on earth. If you are an intention, it means that you are a great idea meant to make a difference on earth. Don't diminish your responsibility by feeling inadequate. Your feeling has nothing to do with your genetics. Your genetics say that you are a fantastic purpose born into the world; go ahead and show the world that you've arrived. Birth that idea!

7. An idea is a scheme or a plan: without a scheme or plan, an idea will remain ambiguous. A scheme or plan gives shape to an idea; a scheme or a plan is the design of the idea. An idea without a scheme or plan has no structure; without a structure, it cannot be developed. A plan is a definite purpose while a scheme is a design, visionary or impractical project.

8. An idea is a conviction: Conviction is a fixed or firm belief, or persuasion. A persuasive idea is an idea based on the foundation of confidence, certainty, principle and reliance. The foundation of confidence, certainty, principle and reliance says; work on your conviction; work on your idea. You don't need another man's approval to follow your heart. You may need a confirmation; someone reiterating what your subconscious has already impressed on you, but I insist; you don't need any man's approval. Some people think that until they give you the go ahead, you should get stuck in mediocrity, but my answer is No; don't do that, go ahead and run the distance meant for your destiny. You are personally accountable for what you do, so, let the final decision come from you. If you leave your life for another man to run, they will drive you into the grave without achieving your purpose on earth. Follow your conviction; follow your idea; make it happen.

9. An idea is perception: perception is insight, immediate or intuitive recognition. Intuition comes by inspiration. Intuitiveness is independent of any reasoning process. For example, it is your intuition that tells you that someone is standing behind you even if, with your five senses, you can't connect with the person.

Sometimes, we trick our mates by sneaking behind them, but somehow, they suddenly turn around to see us, and then make statements like, 'I knew someone was behind me.' How did they know? It was by perception or intuition.

Some ideas are intuitive. Sometimes, solutions to certain challenges come by intuition.

10. An idea is a seed: a seed is that integral part of a plant or animal that produces its young ones. A seed is used for procreation. Just like plants and animals, an idea is a seed. It gives birth to young products and services. These young products and services, if properly developed, expand into huge organisations. Coca Cola was a seed before developing into a multinational organisation. Microsoft was a seed before germinating and expanding into a global company. The little idea in your mind may turn into a global concept if you sow it, cultivate it, and invest it.

How do you generate ideas?

Generating ideas helps you introduce concepts that were not originally in existence. Without new ideas, the world will remain static. New ideas birth new creativities; new creativities make the world a better place to live.

Man was made with the ability to be creative. Creativity begins with the seed called ideas. Everything that was made began with ideas; everything that was created began with ideas. For you to stand out, your ideas must stand out; for your ideas to stand out, you must understand how to generate good ones.

How are ideas generated?

1. By creative thinking: creativity is inspired by stimulation, ingenuity, vision, innovation and invention. Thinking is a type of meditation. Meditation involves a deep pondering, rumination and incubation.

156

Creative thinking helps you generate creative ideas. There are many ways of thinking but I will only be discussing certain methods that I have discovered:

a. Think strategically: strategy is a military terminology. It is the science or art of combining and employing the means of war in planning and directing large military movements and operations. It is the utilisation during both peace and war, of all a nation's forces, through large scale, long range planning and development to ensure security or victory. So, in a more ordinary definition, a strategy is a plan, method or series of manoeuvres for obtaining a specific goal or result.

To think strategically, you must think like a planner and a developer with a specific goal in your mind whether you are involved in a competition or not. You don't need to face opposition for you to think strategically. Whether in peace or war, learn to think strategically. The plans that make you excel come from everyday thinking. Creative thinkers are everyday thinkers. Think purposefully; think strategically.

b. Think tactically: strategy and tactics have very close relationship, but the difference between them is that strategy is utilised during peace and war time while tactics deals with actual combat. In times of competition or opposition, a man's level of thinking must step up. The thinking you embark on when faced with challenges are not strategic but tactical. If you keep thinking strategically in times of warfare, you're not a good leader. Your thinking must go from strategy to tactics when the enemy stands face to face with you.

One of the ways of generating ideas especially in emergency situations is through tactical thinking.

c. Think symbolically: a symbol is something that is used to represent another thing. This may be in form of a sign, emblem, mark, letter, token, figure, character, logo, etc. Thinking symbolically gives you the ability to interpret symbols.

157

Certain marks represent some things; without thinking symbolically, you can't get into their depths. A strategic or tactical thinker that does not think symbolically will not understand the meaning of a sign when he approaches it. Therefore, study emblems, letters, tokens, figures, etc, so that you can understand what they stand for. Understanding what they represent will broaden your ability to creatively generate ideas.

d. Think figuratively: thinking figuratively helps you create figures of speech like using words metaphorically. A metaphor, for instance is a figure of speech in which a term or phrase is applied to something to which it is not literally applicable in order to suggest a resemblance. For example, the sentence 'She reasons like a star' is metaphorical because in real sense, nobody is a star. Thinking figuratively is one excellent avenue of enhancing creative writing. If you want to stand out as a writer or communicator, you must learn to think figuratively.

e. Think descriptively: description gives an account of something either through writing or spoken word. To describe, you must build up your vocabulary and terminology. To describe, you must understand structures because if you don't notice and understand shapes and structures, you won't be able to describe. Description must take notice of milestones; milestones are certain unforgettable junctions or points. For example, if you're asked to describe the way you wrote an article, how would you approach it? Thinking descriptively will help you put an easy structure and shape to your creative ideas. If you have an idea but cannot describe it, no one can step into the inner recesses of your heart to pull out what you're thinking.

f. Think narratively: narration has a close relationship with description. Description gives skeletal information while narration gives the detail information. To have thorough knowledge, you need the details. To develop ideas, you need the details. So, learn to think narratively.

g. Think logically: logic is the pattern, system and principle of reasoning used in a specific subject or field. For instance, Mathematicians reason in a specific way. Doctors have their line of reasoning, just like accountants also have theirs. If doctors reason like accountants, patients will die in the hospitals. To generate great ideas, you must think in line with the system of reasoning inclined to your endeavour. Logic analyses patterns of reasoning by which a conclusion is properly drawn from a set of premises, without reference to meaning or context. Premises are propositions supporting or helping to support a conclusion. If your point or argument doesn't make sense, it is not a good premise. If it is not a good premise, it is not logical. For example, if someone asks, 'What is the colour of air?' Simply saying that air is colourless is not logical. On what premise is your answer based? Answering that air is colourless because it is not visible to the naked eyes even when viewed under a microscope is more logical. Without logic, you cannot convince people to accept your line of thinking over certain subjects. So, there are certain instances that logic will help you create some innovative ideas. Think logically!

h. Think proactively: taking action before the event occurs is proactivity. Proactivity begins with anticipation. A person with keen vision sees it before it happens. He therefore, plans to either make the event occur, if it is good, or stop it from occurring if it is bad. A person who is a proactive thinker has foresight. In leadership, proactive thinkers make better leaders because they take advantage of foresight to change or manipulate future occurrences. For example, a stock broker who is proactive can anticipate the rise or fall of certain share values in the stock market, and then act responsibly to make profits or avoid losses. Thinking proactively is a preventative strategy. To anticipate and prevent, you must generate ideas that will put you on the winning side rather than on a losing side. Those who don't think proactively get caught by the web of eventualities.

i. Think reactively: no matter how proactive we are, some events still catch us unaware. For example, if you have an appointment at 10.00 am, no matter how much you try to beat the time, you may not be able to beat the traffic because it is not within your control. How do you deal with uncontrollable variables? Your quick response will give you an edge in dealing with such unforeseen circumstances. The way you react to events that are sudden is determined by your ability to think reactively. You should realise that reaction is measured by spontaneity. How spontaneous are you when confronted by issues you didn't bargain for? If you're too slow, you will lose your deals. If you're too hasty, you will outrun your deals. None of these approaches are good for your business. You must learn to strike a time balance as you react to unforeseen circumstances. Thinking reactively generates ideas that help deal with emergencies. Your type of reaction determines how good you are in making quality decisions. Quality decisions define excellent leadership.

j. Think globally: anyone who thinks globally thinks up, down, right and left. Thinking up is thinking north, thinking down is thinking south while thinking right and left is thinking west and east. Understanding the global culture will help you generate global ideas. There are certain organisations that have broken into different regions of the world because they understand different global cultures. Ideas for international marketing are based on global thinking. If you're too regional in your thoughts, your business, talent, or pursuits will remain regional. Think globally; it pays to think globally!

2. By Market Research: one major source of idea generation is through market research. According to www.studententerprise.ie, market research is the process of collecting valuable information to help you find out if there is a market for your proposed product or services. But the American Marketing Association defines it as the systematic gathering, recording and analysing of data about problems relating to the marketing of goods and services.

160

Market research encompasses qualitative and quantitative research. Qualitative research is non-numeric research; you cannot assign figure to it. For example, you can't measure colour, because it doesn't come in numeric. Quantitative research is numerical research; you can measure or count it. For example, you can count the number of apples in a supermarket.

Having said that, how does market research help in idea generation? After eight years of interviewing people in many areas of England, I have come to realise that the major way of generating ideas in market research is through open-ended questionnaires. Open-ended questions allow you to probe the respondent until he releases all the information he has within regarding the subject of interest. If for example, I ask, 'Can you tell me all the supermarkets you've done your grocery shopping in the last 5 years?' It may be easy for the respondent to answer if he uses a limited number of supermarkets. If I further ask, 'What are your reasons for using those supermarkets?' The respondent may give me one or two reasons. But with one or two reasons, I can't really get to the bottom of why he uses those supermarkets. In order to dig into him, I will have to probe him by asking more questions. I may say, 'Apart from the reasons you just gave to me, what further reasons can you tell me for using those supermarkets?' When he gives me more, I can further ask, 'Anything else?' In asking more and more questions on the same issue, I am probing him, and by probing, more ideas and information emanate. In all honesty, probing is the best method of generating ideas in market research.

In focus group interviews, open-ended questions are used. In drafting personal development questionnaires, open-ended questions are very useful because they put the individual in control of their destinies. By doing this, the person involved is able to think and unleash ideas that are intrinsic and original.

Some people don't ponder until they're made to, or sometimes pushed to. So, by probing further using open-ended questions, their brains are put to work. It will surprise you how much innovative ideas will come out of a person if he is put under measurable pressure through probing.

3. By accident: accident is not only fatal, there are good accidents. If you accidentally stumble on something worthwhile, it becomes a good accident. There are certain creative ideas that were not pre-planned, people stumbled on them. Some scientific breakthroughs were not originally planned, but while scientists were busy searching for something else, those ideas surfaced. In science.discovery.com, some scientific accidental discoveries were highlighted.

a. The discovery of penicillin: Alexander Fleming didn't clean up his workstation before going on vacation one day in 1928. When he came back, Fleming noticed that there was a strange fungus on some of his cultures. Even stranger was that bacteria didn't seem to thrive near those cultures. Penicillin became the first and is still one of the most widely used antibiotics.

b. The discovery of artificial cardiac pacemaker: artificial cardiac pacemaker is a medical device that uses electrical impulses, delivered by electrodes contacting the heart muscles, to regulate the beating of the heart. This device was discovered by accident. The pacemaker was discovered because an American engineer, Professor Wilson Greatbatch reached into his box and pulled out the wrong resistor. He was working on a circuit that will help record fast heart sounds. He put his hand into his box but instead of bringing out 10,000 ohm resistor, he brought out 1 mega-ohm one. The circuit he ended up designing pulsed for 1.8 milliseconds and then stopped for 1 second. This pulse and stop kept on repeatedly like the perfect heartbeat of man. It was based on the accidental circuit that the artificial cardiac pacemaker was designed.

c. **The discovery of mauve:** in 1856, the Chemist, William Perkin wanted to produce quinine used in curing malaria, instead, he accidentally made mauve. The substance he produced was a thick murky mess, but this mess had a beautiful colour. This beautiful mess became the first ever synthetic dye. Later, Paul Ehrlich inspired by Perkin's dye pioneered immunology and chemotherapy used in curing cancer.

d. **The discovery of radioactivity:** in 1896, Henri Becquerel was fascinated by two things: natural fluorescence and the newfangled X-ray. He ran a series of experiments to see if naturally fluorescent minerals produced X-rays after they had been left out in the sun. One problem - he was doing these experiments in the winter, and there was one week with a long stretch of overcast skies. He left his equipment wrapped up together in a drawer and waited for a sunny day. When he got back to work, Becquerel realized that the uranium rock he had left in the drawer had imprinted itself on a photographic plate without being exposed to sunlight first. There was something very special about that rock. Working with Marie and Pierre Curie, he discovered that that something was radioactivity.

e. **The discovery of plastic:** In 1907 shellac was used as insulation in electronics. It was costing the industry a pretty penny to import shellac, which was made from Southeast Asian beetles, and at home chemist Leo Hendrik Baekeland thought he might turn a profit if he could produce a shellac alternative. Instead his experiments yielded a moldable material that could take high temperatures without distorting. Baekeland thought his "Bakelite" might be used for phonograph records, but it was soon clear that the product had thousands of uses. Today plastic, which was derived from Bakelite, is used for everything from telephones to iconic movie punch lines.

f. **The discovery of vulcanised rubber:** one day, Charles Goodyear mistakenly spilled a mixture of rubber, sulphur and lead onto a hot stove. The heat charred the mixture but didn't ruin it because it was heat and cold resistant. When he picked up the charred mixture, he noticed that it was hardened but still usable. That charred hardened mixture is vulcanised rubber used in making tyres, shoes, etc.

g. The discovery of coke: Atlanta Pharmacist John Pemberton was trying to find a cure for headaches when his mixture which is still a close guarded secret turned into coke. Today, Coca Cola is a household name in every nation on earth.

h. The discovery of smart dust: Jamie Link was doing her doctoral work in chemistry at the University of California, San Diego, when one of the silicon chips she was working on burst. She discovered afterward, however, that the tiny pieces still functioned as sensors. The resulting "smart dust" won her the top prize at the Collegiate Inventors Competition in 2003. These teensy sensors can also be used to monitor the purity of drinking or seawater, detect hazardous chemical or biological agents in the air, or even to locate and destroy tumour cells in the body.

i. The discovery of saccharin: Saccharin, the sweetener in the pink packet, was discovered because chemist Constantin Fahlberg didn't wash his hands after a day at the office. The year was 1879 and Fahlberg was trying to come up with new and interesting uses for coal tar. After a productive day at the office, he went home and something strange happened. He noticed the rolls he was eating tasted particularly sweet. He asked his wife if she had done anything interesting to the rolls, but she hadn't. They tasted normal to her. Fahlberg realized the taste must have been coming from his hands -- which he hadn't washed. The next day he went back to the lab and started tasting his work until he found the sweet spot.

4. By necessity: necessity is something needed for a desired result. Necessity is a requirement, fundamental and obligation. It is an imperative and compulsion; something that demands urgent and non-urgent attention.

Most inventions that took place in the world came out of needs. When there is a specific need, curious minds look for solutions. Curious minds are philosophical minds. The ideas that have ruled the world and still rule the world came out of curiosity.

Fluoride toothpaste was a need; it helped strengthen the teeth and made them healthier. The seat-belt was a need; it helped increase the safety of passengers in motor vehicles. The Global Positioning System (GPS) was a need; it navigates you to your destination with ease. The search engine Google was a need; it makes your search easy on the internet. The internet was a need; I wonder what the modern day life would be without it. The computer was a need; the world will be a million years backward without it. The black box was a need; air crash investigations would be inconclusive without it. I can go on and on. Without these needs, ideas to meet them will not come up. One of the best ways of generating ideas is responding to needs. Whenever there's a response, there's an answer. Answers are creative ideas in creative minds.

5. By meditative reading: If you are meditative reader, you will discover that as you read, you stop, ponder and continue reading. Pondering helps you chew the information you're reading. By pondering on any point that strikes your mind, somehow, new information rushes into your mind. You can generate a new idea from another person's information if you know how to read. I do appreciate speed reading but I don't like it because it doesn't give you the privilege to stop and ponder. Where you can't chew the information, you can't bring innovation to the information.

6. By using the subconscious: the psychologists call it subconscious but I prefer calling it the spirit man because I believe that man is a tripartite being; he is a spirit, has a soul and lives inside the body. When a man dies, it is his spirit that leaves his body. The soul is the intellectual part of man but the

165

spirit is the real man. In the spirit of man is abundance of creative ideas. If a man can learn how to listen to his spirit, he will stand out in generating creative ideas. How do you know the difference between your spirit and soul? I will use a very simple illustration. Sometimes, when you're standing or staring towards a specific direction, somehow, something in you tells you that there's someone standing behind you. When you turn and see a friend who tiptoed towards you from behind, you laugh and say, 'Somehow, I knew there was someone behind me'. How did you know? It was your spirit or subconscious that alerted you; it wasn't your soul. The soul needs the five senses; touch, smell, taste, sight and sound to give you information, but your spirit or subconscious doesn't. Whether asleep or awake, your subconscious gives you quality innovative ideas if you learn to listen. I have personally received some information that I have written on some of my books from my subconscious; sometimes, these information are from my sleep in dreams. I have received a few quotes from my dreams and subconscious. One of the quotes I specifically remember is 'For the fact you can shake my waist does not mean you can move my weight'.

7. By brainstorming: brainstorming is a conference technique of solving specific problems, amassing information, stimulating creative thinking, developing new ideas, etc; by unrestrained and spontaneous participation in discussion. If a group of people deliberately sit down to search for solution to a specific problem, they will come up with pools of ideas from which a conclusion can be drawn. Some strategic leadership ideas come from brainstorming.

8. By using ideas generation software: currently, technology has made it easy to generate certain ideas by using some types of software. For example, idea management software helps you create management ideas and share them. As technology keeps improving, there will be more software that will be developed for the purpose of generating marvelous and incredible ideas.

So, don't turn a blind eye to technology; open your eyes to see how it can help you generate the relevant information you need to succeed in your area of endeavour.

9. Go back to the dump: there are certain ideas generated in the past that were abandoned because people thought they were practically impossible to achieve, but some of the things that were impossible yesterday are now possible today. Except you go into the past to find out what was in the past, you may lose valuable ideas that were dumped in history. To move on in a specific subject or endeavour, know its history. History will help you realise what was forgotten but may be useful today. Don't throw away yesterday because it is the foundation of today. Don't throw away today because it is the foundation of tomorrow. There are lots of ideas hidden in yesterday that were not used; find them, polish them, and use them.

10. The use of music: music is the easiest way to subtly pass information to someone. When music hits the soul, it triggers unusual inspiration. The inspiration triggered by music can make a person conceive an idea. If the music is good, it triggers the conception of quality ideas, but if it is bad, heinous ideas will be conceived. Music and mathematical formulas work together. Mathematical ideas can be generated when soft inspirational music is being played.

11. The use of experts: specialist ideas are generated only by specialists. If you don't know the subject, you can't generate ideas in the subject. There are topics that are no go areas for people who are not skilled in those areas, and for such, leave it for experts to discuss and come up with useful solutions or ideas that will deal with such challenges. For example, the idea needed to redesign aircraft engines don't come from laymen, they come from those who have the expertise skill. The idea to be more successful in performing heart surgeries don't come from mechanical engineers, they come from heart surgeons. Everyone that has been trained has his scope of operation; therefore, he can easily manipulate his skill in order to come up with purposeful ideas that will make life better. So, if you don't know it, leave it for the experts.

How to develop ideas

Many people have generated ideas but haven't developed them. Everyone has one or two ideas that will make him succeed, but how many people have stepped beyond idea stage to reach for its actualisation? Just like a viable seed, if you don't sow it, you can't make it fruitful; to make an idea fruitful and useful, you must sow it. Sowing it develops it; developing it makes it manifest. What are the stages involved in idea generation?

1. Sort your ideas: on a specific issue, there may be multiple ideas that you've generated; you need to sort them. Sorting them involves narrowing down the ideas to the specific and most important one that you need, that is, the one that will give you the best result. To sort, you must put all your cards on the table, and ask yourself some specific and purposeful questions about what you really need. It is your need that must define your choice; if there is no need, don't make the choice. Any alternative you pick outside need will come back to hunt you. When you sort the ideas, don't follow popular opinions; follow purposeful opinions. After all said and done, purpose will always win the game.

2. Create the picture of your choice idea on your mind: the best place to draw the picture of your destination is your mind. When travelling, even if you've never been to that city, you always have a picture of your destination on your mind. Seeing the picture of your destination makes you focus on your journey; you can't focus on what you can't see. Always see the picture of your idea; carry it everywhere you go. The ability to create and continue seeing the picture is what makes you a visionary; visionaries always see their ends from their beginnings.

3. Perfect the picture of your choice idea on your mind: the more you see something, the more you understand what you see. Understanding what you see makes you know the areas of it that need to be worked on. Ideas are not usually perfect from inception; the more you look at them, the more you tidy them up. Working on an impure idea will not do you any good, so, constantly and daily behold the picture you're carrying on your mind in order to make it cleaner and better. As you spot anomalies in your choice idea, reshape and restructure them in the inner recesses of your heart. For example, sometimes, if I want to write on a specific subject, I brood on the ideas that will make up the subject for days, weeks or even months before going ahead to write. By doing that, I perfect the information before externally putting it down. This strategy is applicable in all spheres of idea development; don't rush into it if you've not brooded on it. Constantly visit and behold it so that you can perfect it.

4. Put the design on paper: a design that is not on paper has resigned. Anyone that resigns loses his position and employability. No one can physically produce an idea that is not on paper. If you don't spell out what you have inside, it cannot be given an external resemblance. So, put on paper what you're seeing inside in order for it to be produced outside. It can't be useful to anyone if it only resides inside you. If you cannot design it, say it to those who can; let them design or write it down. We don't always have the skill to write or design what we have inside, but at least, we can say what we have inside. Put your design on paper!

5. Let someone else look at the design: when I say someone else, I mean someone trustworthy. Be careful who you let into your dream because letting a wrong person in can turn it into nightmare. Having said that, you still need to let a second or third eye behold what you've been beholding. Other people have the ability to see what you cannot see. Granting an external person access into your idea can help perfect your idea.

169

The person may take out something that gives your idea an imperfect shape; he may also add something to make it better, or confirm the perfection of what you've done. Any of these actions or contributions will go a long way increasing the quality of your idea. To develop your idea, get involved, people that have eyes; visionary people.

6. Accept constructive criticisms: don't make excuses for imperfections; simply change them. If a criticism is right, accept it. Some people don't accept that they're ever wrong even when it's obvious that they are. Accepting constructive criticism is a great attribute of success. If it is rightly observed, admit it.

7. If necessary, adjust your design based on the constructive criticism: it is not enough to accept a constructive criticism; use it. Use it to correct the design; use it to adjust it in order to perfect it. To develop your idea, never throw away good advice.

8. Make a prototype: a prototype is a mock of the design; it is not the main product but a resemblance of the main product. A prototype will give you an idea of how the final product will look like. For example, when an office or a shopping complex is about to be constructed, the engineers usually make a prototype of the complex for them to see how the final building will look like. I am of the opinion that every idea that requires development must have a prototype.

9. Display the prototype: displaying the prototype is for three major reasons; analysis, impression and further constructive criticism. Analysis, because as you work on your project, you should be able to examine the details of your idea in order to discover its true meaning and relevance. Furthermore, the more you see your prototype, the more it impresses a great and beautiful picture on your mind. This impression becomes a driving force that pushes you to complete it. In terms of constructive criticism, if the prototype is publicly displayed, people can see it and make positive comments that may be useful in perfecting your idea.

10. Adjust the prototype where possible: when a prototype is displayed and analysed, additional ideas may surface. Don't turn a blind eye to fresh and more useful information; use them. Use them to adjust the design; use them to adjust the prototype. Don't lay your bed with the blanket of rigidity; embrace change.

11. Be a producer: don't die on prototypes; be a producer. Go ahead and make it happen. Go ahead and make the product. Don't spend your whole life designing what you're not producing. It can't be useful if it is not produced. It can't bless you if it is not produced. It can't make you if it is not produced. It can't give you money if it is not produced. Produce it, so that it can produce for you the wealth you're looking for.

12. Test the product: an untested product is a potential hazard. Don't take it to the market until you've tested it; and that is the reason you should produce less quantity at the initial stage. For example, when you self publish a book, it is advisable to print a small quantity in order to test the market. Apart from testing the market, you may find some typographical errors in the initial print, so, it saves you a huge cost to print less numbers in case errors are discovered. In other forms of products, product tests are carried out with consumers in form of market research in order to find out people's opinions. So, don't sell an untested product because if consumers find out the errors you either didn't discover or covered up, it may not be easy to win back their trusts. After testing the product, the wise thing to do is make corrections before making further productions. When the loosed ends are tightened, the sky will be your limit!

13. Consistently do a post-market research: no matter how successful your product is in the market, constantly carry out post market research. Post market research is the type of research carried out when the product is already in the market. Major organisations like Coca Cola, Apple, Samsung, etc; regularly carry out post market research. These big organisations have yearly budgets for conducting market researches. If you want to be in the vanguard of successful organisations, you must not undermine the power of market research. If you want your idea to have a cutting edge, you must continuously search for ways of making it better.

The idea of today may become dated tomorrow if it is not regularly updated. In these days of cutting edge technology, people from different parts of the world are coming up with super and better ideas; you can't afford to sleep because you generated and developed an idea that took over the market a few months or years ago. You must not just stand on your feet but on your toes in order to be in the frontline.

CHAPTER TEN

HOW ICONS MOTIVATE THEMSELVES

As a Premiership football fan, I enjoy watching matches and also derive fun from the actions and the anthems, so to say, of the different clubs. I am not a Liverpool Football Club supporter, but I do love their song; 'You'll never walk alone.' In spite of liking that song, I have come to realise that sometimes, either by purpose or destiny, you will have to walk alone. When you are abandoned by the roadside, and you actually want to get to your destination, you will have to walk alone. When no one believes in where you're going except you, you will have to walk alone. When every attempt you have made to succeed fails, and everyone that once believed in you gives up hope that your dream is worth fighting for, you will have to walk alone. Icons sometimes walk alone because the dreamland they're heading to goes through the tunnels of failure before reaching the city of achievement. At the city of success, everyone will celebrate you, but before getting there, I'm sorry, you'll have to walk alone.

At the junction of loneliness, how do you carry on? At the point where it appears like you're the only one on earth, abandoned and confused, how do you find enough courage to keep fighting for your dream? Self-motivation is essential for resuscitation if you must reach that place you envision in the remote areas of your heart. There are days of deflation; so many days indeed. There are years of diffusion; too many beyond numeric. Except you stand up for your life, no one will stand for you. Many times, I have heard people say, 'stand up and be counted', but many have stood, and yet weren't counted. So, I tell people, 'stand up and be counted, but keep standing even if they don't count you.' The reason I say that is because, come to think of it, who does the counting, and what are the criteria for being counted? The one who does the counting determines the rules, and if they don't like your face, they won't count you no matter how qualified you are. It is your responsibility to count yourself in, so, make the rules of inclusivity and exclusivity; determine your in-or-out, and don't give a damn who doesn't like it. You were created to be outstanding; there's no other life to do it beyond the one you're living; there is no other world to showcase your talent beyond this same world. It's your time, make good use of it.

How do you motivate yourself? To motivate yourself,

You must be hopeful: hope is the belief in possibilities. It is the inner conviction that what is wanted can be had, and that events will turn out for the best in spite of what the situation currently is. Hope is the inner picture of future victory.

Without hope, a man may be physically alive, but futuristically dead. You can't help a man that refuses to believe in hope. You can't give life to someone that doesn't see life, tomorrow. To be self motivated, first have hope; despite the odds, be bold to see something better ahead of you. Seeing something better ahead gives you life; those who see the future, live in the future.

You must behold the outcome: hope and outcome appear similar but I will give you the thin line difference between both. Hope tells you that there will be positive result; outcome tells you the quality and quantity of the value of the result. Knowing the quantity of the value you will get from something motivates you to carry on. For instance, if you are a student, your hope is that one day after graduating, you will get a certificate, but it doesn't tell you the grade. Beholding a first class gives you inner fire to aspire when you are completely tired. That is the outcome!

To self-motivate, you must keep seeing the outcome. If you don't see the outcome, you will go for anything. Beholding the outcome puts you on fire to do more than the usual; it helps you to go beyond average.

Recreate your environment: your environment is where you live; your apartment, office, car, etc. There is a connection between your environment and your life. Environments are either healthy or unhealthy; they are either living or dying; they are either succeeding or failing. Whatever your environment poses, you have the power to recreate it.

How can you recreate your environment? Your eyes, ears, nose, skin, and tongue determine what goes into your inner system. Whatever your brain processes is determined by your five senses. Whatever is processed by your brain goes into your mind, and whatever goes into your mind has access into your spirit. Your spirit determines your life or death. So, you must be mindful what you see, hear, touch, smell and taste. The pictures in your environment are either life or death. The music, sounds, or gossips you listen to are life or death. So are the issues related to touch, smell and taste. If you display a picture that denotes fear in your home, your brain processes it, and sends it to your spirit, and your spirit will give back to you exactly what you've ingested. If you keep listening to sad and horrible news, your brain also processes it, and passes it to your spirit. Your spirit will equally give you back in multiples what you've ingested. On the other hand, if you display positive and healthy images, and listen to inspiring and motivating music, information and read life enhancing books, you will get exactly the outcome of your input. You see, you are responsible for creating your environment through your decision making processes. Some murderers created the scene through watching horrific movies, listening to some terrible music, and so on, before executing the act. Most successful people recreated their environments before succeeding by engaging with successful environments.

Keep quality relationships: there is morale boost in seeing some people. There is also a deflation of morale when you come in contact with certain people. Relationship can be motivating or demotivating. Some people encourage you to stand up when you're down; others mourn with you in your state of downtrodden, they hardly show you the way up, that is, if they know at all. Some people make you happy by helping you see the positive side of things while others deepen your sadness by opening your eyes to see how bad your adversaries have ruined you. You may walk alone sometimes, but the great words of positive people will keep reverberating on your mind. Even when you walk alone, good people will be on the sideline to cheer you to victory. As you go on vision road, quality relationship is a major key that will help you succeed.

Go window shopping: people hardly realise the power of window shopping when dispirited. It helps change your environment, and makes you breathe some fresh air.

I remember when for some years, my family and I went through a torrential moment in life. In order to ease tension, sometimes, my wife and I will take a walk to some beautiful shops for window shopping. We didn't have the money to buy, but we would go and admire the beauties of life and with that, our minds were always beautiful. It's a moment I will never forget, but in those moments, in spite of our financial distress, I wrote about nine books. Window shopping, in moments of difficulties, help elevate your spirit, and gives you the hope of a better tomorrow. You may not be able to buy, but it costs you nothing to see and dream. What you dream, you will eventually get.

Window shopping doesn't just mean going to shops. If your challenge is poor health, shop around healthy people. If yours is unemployment, go to the city where there are mega offices; shop around them; dream. Whatever your challenge is, go window shopping!

Resist, insist, and persist: as you walk through the valley of the shadow of death, resist being a victim. So many people have become victims to failures because they crumbled easily when the situation appeared like the end of the road. At the end of every road is an opportunity to construct a new one. The road is only ended when you think it is, so, the end of the road is only in your imagination. Resist being stuck. Make a way, even if there isn't one.

Insist on making it to the main event. You weren't born to always be in the dark. Be a fighter; don't fall like a pack of cards. Fight your way through the obstacles that tend to stop you. Don't give up; don't give in. It may not be working out, but don't walk out. It is your insistence that will give you the required result that will produce the difference you want. Insist!

My best definition of persistence is from the Medical Dictionary. It says, 'Persistence is the continuance of an effect after the cause is removed.' This means that, when all forms of motivating factors are no longer there, you still continue with your drive; that is self-motivation without a motivator. You must learn to persist. Maintain your inspiration when every agent of inspiration has abandoned you. That is the attitude of icons. That is how they win.

Learn to meditate: when I talk about meditation, I am not talking about some strange form of practice carried out by certain cults. By meditation, I simply mean setting some time apart each day to be alone so that you can think, ponder and consider or reconsider certain plans, ideas, or innovations. The best time I think is perfect for meditation is early morning. At that time, everywhere is quiet, and you can hear clearly from within. Why do I use the word within? Humans are made up of spirit, soul and body. Your body is your physical self, but your spirit and soul are within; they form your subconscious. Take it or leave it, your spirit and soul know far more than your physical body. If you quieten your physical body by staying away from noise and distractions, your subconscious will guide you into making far more quality decisions than your physical body.

Meditation involves thinking and pondering on ideas; it also helps you generate and sharpen your ideas. For instance, most of the points I write on, I do get in times of meditation.

How does meditation work? Most times, some people have used two keywords to describe meditation; they are incubation and rumination; they both involve animals. For those that live in third world nations especially the countryside of black Africa, they are used to chickens laying eggs and incubating them. While growing up, my maternal grandmother had some hens. They would lay about ten to eleven eggs, and then sit on them for about twenty one days. Sitting on the eggs helps incubate them, until the chicks are formed within the shells. On the twenty first day, the mother hen pecks the shells, and the young chicks will come out.

This action is comparable to meditation. Meditation incubates your ideas as you sit on them, until they move from ideas to realities. The hope that your ideas are undergoing incubation is self motivating.

Examples of ruminants are goats, cows, and sheep; they are plant eating animals. If you've lived close to nature like I have, you will notice how goats feed. When they eat plants, they are able to regurgitate part of what they've eaten especially at night. What they regurgitate is called cuds. They chew these cuds over and over again, and swallow. This, they do often and often.

In comparison to meditation, if you, like ruminants regurgitate your ideas and chew them over and over again, those ideas will work. The mere fact that you're chewing your ideas is enough conviction to give you that self belief that the outcome will be perfect.

Meditation helps you fine tune your ideas and gives you self belief and confidence. Meditation is self motivating!

Practice self talk: practicing self talk is another form of meditation but I deliberately didn't include it on the meditation point so that it won't get lost in the multitude of words. I have found the practice of self talk very useful in life. Practicing self talk helps reaffirm your beliefs; it acts as consolidation.

There are many occasions when you feel like nobody; you have to be able to tell yourself that you're somebody. When you feel like a failure, you should be able to say to yourself that you are successful. Sometimes, when you feel incapable or unable, you should reassure yourself through self talk that you are capable and able. In the midnight of your life, no one will be awake to encourage you; it is up to you to encourage yourself.

Every morning, before my children go to school, I guide them on self talk. I do lead them in making recitations so that it will boost their confidence as they step into their day. I ask them to say things like, 'As I go to school today, I believe in my heart and I confess with my mouth that I am the best. I'm the head, not tail. I am winning everyday, succeeding everyday, and excelling everyday....'

Self talk is reinvigorating and energising. Use it daily, and it will help motivate you.

CHAPTER ELEVEN

HOW TO DEVELOP YOUR SKILLS

There was a man, who trained as an engineer. He was so good, that he made a first class. Everyone called him Mr. Brainy. It didn't take long before many companies started headhunting him. He chose one good one; began to make big money; he was so comfortable. He got married and had two lovely children; a boy and a girl. Everything was simply wow and okay; he had no financial, family or material problems. He stood out among his peers; he was envy to all who knew him. But suddenly, the internet was discovered, and everything started moving from analogue to digital; software became the order of the day. This man was deeply rooted in the analogue system; he found it difficult to change. At first, he played down the direction that the digital age was going, but before he knew it, it was running faster than he thought. His organisation, due to competition, began restructuring to meet the new ways of doing things, but the man got stuck in his dated methodology. In spite of his long years of commitment to the organisation, he was compulsorily retired when he couldn't adapt to change.

Things are changing daily; mono skill is danger to survival. Whatever you were yesterday, you should either expand its knowledge today, or divert into other fields in order to increase your broadness. These days, employers are searching for people with extra factors as the competition for the small job spaces increases daily. Even admissions to some sacred disciplines in Universities, and into certain Universities have not been spared from this high level competition. The other day, I read an interview granted to The Guardian Newspaper by the head of one of the most contested disciplines in a grade A University in United Kingdom on the process of selecting students for the department. He said, first, every potential candidate must score As in the required subjects, and in addition, be able to show the extra factor that makes them eligible for selection. These extra factors include the ability to excellently communicate in written and verbal forms, exhibit some tendency for entrepreneurship and other forms of skills that make them stand out. With this, it is evident that having a mono skill isn't enough to make a man outstanding in this digital age.

I believe that there is a difference between talent and skill. Icons also believe; that is why they endeavour to develop theirs. Talent is a natural ability, but it takes skills to raise its level. For instance, a talented singer requires regular voice training to improve her singing ability. A talented footballer requires the help of a coach to help him bring to light his talent. A talented writer needs the skills of communications to do good writings.

Without developing ones' skills, talent will remain latent. So many talents are latent because they feel talent alone is enough to make things happen, but it isn't. Talent is a deep-seated ability that requires discipline to fully manifest its potentials. That discipline comes from harnessing other forms of skills, which are, one way or the other connected to the talent. A great singer may want to add the skill of playing musical

182

instruments to her nightingale voice. What a wonder it will be, if she can. For example, it is necessary for any talent to add a computer skill to its repertoire of gifts, as it is expedient today, that in any profession that one belongs, computer skill is vital. Somehow, acquiring and developing ones' skill is a must.

Talents do grow; it is development that makes growth a possibility. The difference between a specialist and a general practitioner is development. To stand out in a specific area, you must develop that area. Developing an area gives you the power of consultation. Don't just have a talent, build your talent.

How can you develop your skills?

Know what your talent is: knowing what your talent is, is number one step to developing your skill. Without knowing your talent, you will be running in the wrong direction; it is danger running in the wrong direction because it is counterproductive.

You must know what your natural abilities are, and then, build your future in line with it. Don't develop a career based on what your nature dislikes. If you don't like seeing blood, it is needless becoming a medical doctor. If you don't easily remember dates, it is needless being a historian. Your future must take your genetics into consideration. Your talent is linked to your genetics; follow it.

Live a life based on passion; your destiny, money, peace and satisfaction are enveloped in your passion. If you don't like it, don't do it. Many people do what they don't like, basically because of the money. If what you don't like is what is available to give you cash, set a timetable of when to exit, as you grow what you like. Don't endlessly do the work you don't like. As you earn from what you dislike, use the money to develop yourself in the area of your passion so that you can easily and quickly exit the stage of unwanted career or profession. So, know what your talent is, in order to know what you should develop.

Find out the skills related to your passion: for any job advertised, the employer writes the job descriptions and also, the skills required to carry out the job. For example, if an organisation advertises for social media manager, some of the skills they require are excellent communication, social media analytics and organisational skills. How can you handle the responsibility of creating, implementing, and managing exciting and engaging content without the aforementioned skills? Your skills will help you deal with your responsibilities. You need to find out what they are.

You need to determine the kind of information or skills you need in order to progress your career, profession, business or education. You don't need every skill; you need something that is relevant to your lane, and there are loads of them. If you are a plumber, what are all the skills related to plumbing, whether it is your area of specialisation or not? If you are a secretary, what are all the skills and software related to your job? Determine everything surrounding your pursuit or goal.

Train yourself: don't die in ignorance; train yourself. When you identify where you're weak, strengthen it. Training yourself is self development. Self development helps you sharpen your dull ends; sharpening your dull ends increases your earnings. If you want to earn better, it only requires a few weeks, months, or years to achieve. All it takes is for you to develop the areas of need in your career or profession. You can know it, if you put money and mind in it. Nothing is impossible for a determined person.

In the age of e-learning, there is no excuse not to advance in a chosen endeavour. You can study from home, bus, train, ship or aeroplane; wherever you are, you carry a school with you. Someone may say, 'I don't have the money to pay for the programme?' Listen, you don't need to go to any organised institution to acquire knowledge. There are millions of free information out there that you can begin with. Leverage what is free before going for what isn't. In studying search engine optimisation, I began reading and practicing what other bloggers in that field have written without paying a penny. After that, I signed up to do an online training at $25 monthly.

Apart from schooling, there are many skills that secular education may not teach, but it is up to you to be conscious of your deficiencies, and deliberately work on them. For instance, I know that many times, different textbooks talk about the relevance of interpersonal skills, but can you really learn interpersonal skills without a deliberate decision to realise that to achieve more in life, you need to understand the importance of being at peace with other people? Someone may score a distinction in a course related to interpersonal skills, but in practice, does not know how to relate with other people. It is up to that person to build bridges or shift some boundaries, or probably, as the case may be, entirely remove those boundaries in order to have harmonious relationship with people around. So, training yourself goes beyond reading a book or books, or sitting for examinations. It also involves taking purposeful actions to build personal characters that are directly or indirectly connected with ones' area of pursuit.

Have an open mind: I have talked a lot about having an open mind, but this topic cannot be overemphasised. Many people fail to learn because their minds are locked up with certain biased attitudes. Having an open mind is an attitude of nobility. An open mind explores different methods of doing things, but a rigid mind abhors creativity.

185

An open mind asks questions. An open mind inhales and exhales. Closed minds only inhale but never exhale, and as a result, die of suffocation.

People with open minds are more intelligent because they always come up with fresh ideas. They share ideas, and also learn from other people. In open minds, there are accessible entry and exit routes; they adopt the principle of permeability. Open minds are like ever flowing streams; so, they don't stink. Learning is best achieved through the attitude of open mindedness. Be willing to know; be also willing to share.

Not too long ago, I called one of my uncles that is highly educated. I told him that I was going to send him a text message over certain information, but he said, 'please don't send a text, post a letter because I don't know how to access text messages' Yes, one can understand that he's old because he's already in his eighties, but there are lots of people within my age group that can't send an email, even if they have all the privileges of technology. In organisations, some people fear change because they're not flexible to learn, but without flexibility, development cannot take place. If we all get stuck to yesterday, by today, we'll all be expired. So, programme your mind to have a teachable spirit. That is your first step to development. Don't think you're too old or too dumb to learn; you are only as old as you think.

If need be, be a mentee: a mentee is someone under the instruction or tutorship of a mentor. In my opinion, everyone should be a mentee because somehow, we all have someone that knows more than us in certain areas of our lives. Being a mentee means we can always run to that person to ask certain questions that we don't understand. Your mentor does not have to be your boss; he or she may even be junior to you in age or position.

One day, I took my daughter to our General Practitioner. While attending to us, he dialled a number on the phone and asked the Admin Assistant to come in. When he came, he said to him, 'I still haven't understood this thing. Can you please, once again, teach me how to use it?' He was referring to the medical software used in writing prescriptions for patients. He was the doctor, but the Admin Assistant was his mentor in terms of learning how to use the software. To develop your skill, be a mentee.

Have a reference tool: to be computer literate, invest on buying a computer; that is your reference tool. Whatever you learn, have a material for it, so that you can always go back to revise it. Constant revision makes you master what you've learnt. There must always be something to put you in remembrance of the rudiments of the skills you've acquired. Without reference, you cannot lay a strong foundation of knowledge.

Discipline yourself to practice daily: learning without practicing leaves you only on a theoretical level. Many people can talk a subject but can't do the subject. It isn't skill if you can't do it. When I started learning how to design the interior of a book, what I did was to offer to do other people's books for free. I used their books to perfect my skills. Same thing happened when I was learning how to do copyediting or copywriting; I practiced with other people's works. Now, I charge to do those jobs for people. You need to practice to become perfect in what you do. To discipline yourself, have a timetable; follow it like a religion.

In conclusion, I say, 'stick to your goal, but understand that your goal has many skills linked to it'. Depending on other people always to help you carry out assignments that you should have been able to do on your own won't do you any good. One day, those people may get tired of you. Even if they don't, they may be indisposed at that very moment you need them. What does it cost you to develop a multi-skill? Discipline and commitment; that's the only price you pay.

CHAPTER TWELVE

STRATEGIC NETWORKING; ILLUSTRATED WITH FISHNET AND VOLVOX

Icons don't work in isolation; they believe in people and are interdependent on people. Without a network, stars can't shine; they need the cooperation of the night. There are many skills that go into the design of a product or service. There are many contributions from various sectors required before an offering goes on the shelf. Without these contributions, things won't work. An aeroplane may be designed by some powerful aeronautical engineers, but it takes far more than engineering to make that plane fly. To put it in the air, many professionals from different fields combine their different skills to make it work. In your dreams and visions, you can only succeed if you network. Everyone may not believe in your dream, but in spite of their disbeliefs, you need them to at least make some input into your expectation. The dream to write a book does not mean that you don't need the services of a printer, who does not believe in your book.

To network, you need to have some basic understanding of how it works. That is the purpose for writing the chapter.

Many times, I have heard people and various organisations talk about the importance and power of strategic network. No one can undermine the holistic relevance of networking because no human being or organisation can exist and succeed in isolation. The reason for international trade is because every nation needs each other to excel. No matter how powerful an individual, organisation or nation may be, she cannot be master in and of everything. Therefore, strategic networking is one of the most powerful actions that must be undertaken in order to be outstanding in a pursuit or endeavour.

As essential as strategic networking is, a lot of people are still lost in understanding how it should be run, how it works, and what goes into it. To explain how strategic networking works, I will use two different unrelated approaches. These two different approaches form networks. If you can understand them, you will be able to understand how strategic network should work. I will be using the fishnet and a microorganism called volvox.

FISHNET

Simply speaking, a fishnet is a net for catching fish. They are made from either polyethylene (resins) or nylon; polyethylene and nylon are chemicals. Polyethylenes are easily molded and are resistant to other chemicals. They can be repeatedly softened and hardened by heating and cooling, and are used for many purposes, such as making containers, tubes, and packaging. Nylon is very strong and elastic, and can be formed into fibers, sheets, or bristles. It is used to make fabrics, plastics, and molded products. The picture of fishnet can be found on a latter page of this book.

Based on their material make, fishnets are classified into:

1. High density polyethylene (HDPE) fishnets
2. Nylon mono filament fishnets
3. Nylon multi-filament fishnets.

For those that don't understand, density is compactness, closeness, and the degree to which something is filled, crowded or occupied. Density is also obtuseness or stupidity. Density is synonymous to consistency, frequency and quantity.

Filament is a thread, fibre and a long slender cell. In plants, it is defined as a stalk-like portion of a stamen, supporting the anther.

Features of the fishnet

1. Fishnets are transparent
2. Fishnets are invisible in water
3. Fishnets have low drag resistance
4. Fishnets have high abrasion resistance. Abrasion is scraping or wearing out
5. Fishnets have high tensile strength, which means that they can be stretched and drawn out. Being drawn out means they are ductile. Being ductile is the ability to be made into wire or thread
6. Fishnets have high knot breaking strength. A knot is an interlacing, twining, or looping of a cord, rope, or the like, drawn tight into a knob or lump, for fastening, binding, or connecting two cords together or a cord to something else
7. The mesh size of fishnets ranges from 10mm to 2000mm based on area and method of application. Mesh means, woven, knitted or knotted.
8. In multifilament fishnets, the number applied in the yarn varies between 2 and 36. A yarn is a continuous thread or strand
9. The various types of knots used for fishnet construction are single, double and U-knots
10. The length and width size of fishnets are primarily driven by customers' terms and conditions. These types of fishnets are obtainable in 100mm, 250mm, 500mm, 600mm, and 1000mm of spools.

The relationship between the Fishnet and Strategic Networking

1. A network is a relationship: a relationship is a connection, association or involvement. In every connection, association or involvement, there must be communication, conjunction and correlation. In a relationship, there must also be affiliation, alliance and dependency. This is what goes on in the fishnet. In the fishnet, every thread connects with another thread to form a thicker thread. In the fishnet, every thread aligns with another thread to form a stronger relationship. This is what should happen in strategic networking. If there is no relationship, a network cannot work. It only works when those involved are ready to bring something purposeful into the net. A net cannot be formed when the threads are not willing to form a single uniformed strand.

2. In a network, there must be transparency: transparency is the tendency to allow the passage of light so that any object behind or beyond can be easily seen. So, in a network, nothing must be hidden behind or beyond, that cannot be observed by those involved. If what is behind is shady, it is not a network.

Another meaning of transparency is the ability to be unsophisticated. When involved in a network, you must be ready to climb down from your high horse. One of the setbacks of networking is unnecessary ego and pride. Unnecessary sophistication kills good relationships.

Transparency also means being straightforward, unambiguous, unequivocal, forthright or articulate. In a network, certain diplomacy is hypocrisy. When truth is required, say it. When a situation, circumstance or assignment requires sincerity and honesty, please, be sincere and honest. A good network dies in the absence of truth.

To catch fish, a fishnet must be transparent. The reason for network is to catch multitude of fish. If the net is not transparent, the purpose becomes defeated. It is therefore expedient that in strategic networking, transparency must be a major goal.

3. Just like the fishnet, a network must be invisible in water: fish will avoid the net if they notice the fishnet. The fishnet is in water not to be noticed by what it is supposed to catch. The water is the business environment. The water is the place of profitability. The water is where the customers are. Everything that goes on behind the scene must not be seen by the target market. The network must be transparent to one another but invisible in water. If your behind-the-scene strategies and tactics are easily noticed in the marketplace, you will hardly make profits. For example, most organisations will hardly reveal to the market, their unit cost of production or service unless on very exceptional cases.

4. A network must have a low drag resistance: when a fishnet is too heavy, it adds unnecessary weight to its catch. The weight of a fishnet is the summation of the individual weights of each thread that makes up the net. If the individual weights are high, the total weight of the net will be high. If a high weight net catches a small quantity of fish, dragging the net out of the water becomes difficult.

Flexibility, agility and versatility are required in networking. These three attributes make the network easy and light. These three attributes make the network have a low drag resistance with or without a catch. If you're too heavy to be involved, you'll be too difficult to drag. It is an unimaginable danger to align with a person or organisation that has a high drag resistance because that person or organisation may end up pulling you into the water. Instead of being the fisherman, you become the fish. Heavy weights make you drown especially if you cannot swim. Heavy weights capsize your fishing boat in the middle of the sea. Don't align with them!

5. Each thread in a network must have a high abrasion resistance: The intention of any competitor is to cut off your network because your network is your major source of strength. Where it becomes impossible to cut it off, they wear it out by scraping and scratching it until it breaks down. The competitor always begins its scratch from your weakest link. If all the threads in your net are not abrasion resistant, one after the other, they will wear out. So, without a high abrasion resistance, your network will be worn out. In networking, endeavour to align with people or organisations that are on their own strong, so that your net will not easily break when those who intend to weary it come against your association. Each thread must be strong in order to produce a good net. If a part of the net is weak and broken, any catch you make will escape through it.

6. Like every good fishnet, a network must have a high tensile strength: to test your genuineness and strength, you will be stretched. If you cannot withstand a stretch, you cannot carry a reasonable weight. Not only should you be able to withstand a stretch, you must have the ability to be drawn out. Being drawn out means being ductile or the ability to be made into a wire. If you can be made into a wire or thread, you have the tendency to connect. If you can be made into a wire or thread, you may also have the ability to conduct. The wires that are metals can conduct electricity. Electricity is power; it is energy; it is illumination.

A good network has a high tensile strength. A good network can be stretched without breaking or becoming brittle. A good network can easily connect and conduct. A good network is power and energy to those involved in it. A good network is illumination.

7. Like fishnets, a network must have a high knot breaking strength: when two wires or threads are tied together, the point of contact forms a knot; the tighter the knot, the stronger the bond. The strength of the bond is determined by the closeness of the wires or threads. Proximity is the power of networking. When two threads are tightly joined together, it becomes very difficult to break, loose or separate them.

Every good network must have a high knot breaking strength, which means, the strength required to break the knot or their knots must be unimaginably high.

8. A good network must be able to determine the size of the strength of its bond: Knowing that you have strength isn't enough; you must know the size of your strength. Your ability to determine the size of your strength makes you accountable. Accountability is an attitude of excellence in networking. In a fishnet for instance, the mesh size of fishnets ranges between 10mm to 2000mm based on area and method of application. Mesh means, woven, knitted or knotted, which means that the mesh is the point or region of contact. A mesh is also the region of correspondence, coordination, harmony and combination. Knowing the size of your correspondence, coordination, harmony or combination is very vital in maintaining your network. How do you do that? Determining the size of the strength of the bond in a network can be assessed through (a) understanding the ease of arriving at a mutual agreement over pressing issues (b) the ease and promptness of responding to communications (c) the respect factor; how much you, your opinions and contributions are valued by your network, (d) the speed of implementation of strategic plans and ideas, etc.

9. A good network does not have arbitrary number of strands: in multifilament fishnet for instance, the number applied in the yarn varies between 2 and 36. A yarn is a continuous thread or strand.

To network, you must determine the number of links you want to have. Determining the number of links makes you carefully select quality and valued links, since you know that you have a limited number. Don't open up to every link. It isn't wise to do so. Connecting with every strand can make you stranded. Some links lead to leaks; be careful. I do understand that keeping it close is keeping it neat and clean. When a net is too big, it can't catch anything purposeful. When a net is too large, it becomes difficult to manage. Anything that cannot be easily managed is susceptible to anarchy.

10. Your network must be relevant to your assignment: The length and width size of fishnets are primarily driven by customers' terms and conditions. These types of fishnets are obtainable in 100mm, 250mm, 500mm, 600mm, and 1000mm of spools. It is the customer that decides the size of its net based on the function it is required for. A net for catching prawns and crabs cannot have the same size with that used in catching big fish.

Just like a fishnet, the length and width of a network must be customer driven. When I use the word, customer, I'm being a bit careless with it because I speak in a metaphoric term. A customer could be anybody or anything whose need has to be met in order to keep your business or relationship going. So, your network must be relevant to your assignment. A thread that is irrelevant to a net will cause it to easily break. Breakage causes loss of values. Some breakage causes irreparable and irreplaceable damage.

What drives your network? What value is your network bringing into your life, career, business or calling? If the thread is irrelevant to your business, keep it at a platonic level.

VOLVOX

If there is any organism whether micro or macro that should be used as illustration for explaining the power of strategic networking, I think volvox should be number one. Volvox is a green alga belonging to the genus chlorophytes. For those without science background, I wouldn't like to bore you with some tongue twisting scientific names, but as I begin to compare the features and characteristics of volvox with strategic networking, you will come to respect this microscopic but very important organism. The picture of Volvox can be found on a latter page of this book.

The relationship between volvox and strategic networking

1. A good network must have a global inclination: volvox is spherical in shape. Its shape is like a globe; the shape of the earth. On its spherical shape are a front end (North Pole) and a rear end (South Pole). These North and South poles are very significant to the organism as they form part of its ability to relate with its environment.

In the same vein, a strategic network must have a global shape. Any network that does not envision the world as its target market is limited in purpose. When I talk about the world as a target market, it doesn't necessarily have to be everyone on earth. The reality of a network is that in every nation, there are people with your type of mentality; whether lifestyle, business, calling, career or entrepreneurial mentality. Being open-minded independent of where the strands that make up your network come from, is key to achieving excellence in your pursuit. Any organisation with a global mindset is always ahead of those that are not ready for change.

2. In spite of large size, a good network must have uniform connective strands binding it together: a typical volvox has about 50,000 individual alga networked together. Each individual alga is connected to the other by a thin strand of cytoplasm. A volvox never breaks its strands; it stays connected in spite of its huge number.

The ability to stay connected in spite of huge size is a reflection of true leadership strength. There must be strands linking each member of the network to the other. Each of these strands must have functional passages for easy access. A strand without a walk-able passage will make those involved in the network stranded. The strands that join different alga in a volvox are functional, that is why there is unity of purpose and vision. For a strategic network to have unity of purpose and vision, it must have functional, passable and walk-able strands.

3. A strategic network must move in a coordinated fashion: when volvox swims, the whole colony move in a coordinate fashion or style. No individual member of a volvox is left behind during movement; they all move together.

In a network, if truly it's a network, no individual member must be left behind. If one moves forward, all must move forward. If one withdraws, all must withdraw. As large as the volvox network is, it is still able to coordinate its movement in a strategic and progressive manner. If leaders, managers and supervisors can learn from volvox, leadership will be easier to manage. Volvox; a microorganism, can synchronise its network in order to ensure that there is order and equality in rank or importance. Man, with his highly developed brain should be able to do far better. Unfortunately, a lot of external factors artificially made and introduced by man into strategic networking make it difficult for man to attain the level and height of networking achieved by volvox.

4. A strategic network must be visionary: earlier, I explained that volvox is spherical in shape, and that it has the front end (North Pole) and the rear end (South Pole). What I didn't mention is that on the front end, volvox has multiples of small red eyespots. With the multiple small red eyespots, it moves towards the direction of light. Light is a symbol of information, knowledge, understanding and revelation. Anyone and anything that moves towards light is interested in vision. Vision sees ahead and plans ahead. Vision is proactive; it takes actions before the event actually occurs. A person that is proactive is a pro. A pro does not just reflect the support of a progressive movement, but is also indicative of someone who is a professional. A true professional is a visionary. A true professional is pro-active.

A strategic network must be visionary. A strategic network must be quality information driven. A strategic network must be knowledge based.

5. In spite of equality, there must be leadership in strategic networking: in spite of the fact that all the members of the colony of volvox are equal, they still have the front and the rear ends. It is foolish and backward not to have leadership. Where there is no leadership, there is no direction. The leadership in a network must be in front. Being in front means taking the hit and heat on behalf of the network. Again, anyone that is in front must, like the volvox have multiples of red eyespots, i.e. must be visionary. Anyone in front in a network must have the agility and readiness to move towards quality information and positive change.

6. A good network should be able to withstand harsh conditions: the zygote (a zygote is a fertilised egg that produces an offspring) of the volvox has the ability to withstand harsh conditions during winter, and so, survives the freezing cold weather.

Just like the zygote of volvox, a good network should be capable of withstanding harsh conditions. The harsh conditions may be difficult business environments, harsh regulatory policies, tough decisions, etc. Developing a tough skin is essential in making a good network work. In networking, every condition is not favourable. The willingness and ability to adapt to changing circumstances are vital in excelling in a network. If you can withstand the harsh weather, you will end up enjoying the good weather.

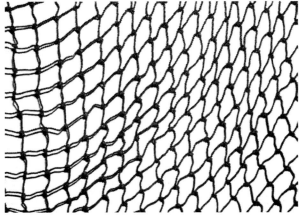

Picture of Fishnet taken from photobucket

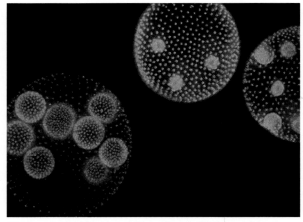

Picture of Volvox taken from Wikipedia

CONCLUSION

Change comes by purposeful deliberate actions, and purposeful deliberate actions come through emancipating knowledge. To rip the cover of ignorance, taking the right steps is a must. To break the chains of failure, adhering to success principles is a must. You can't leave where you are, except you take bold steps to do something different. It may not, at first appear to be working, but your insistence and persistence will drive you through the debacles that want to stop you. You are unstoppable if you courageously keep going when everything says you should stop. Life may bring its hurts, but don't let that confine you to the state of discomfort. There is nothing comfortable with failure; endeavour to succeed. There is no good news in being a loser; you weren't born to lose.

Never conclude that in your pursuit, you are a victim; get up and be a victor. Winning wasn't meant for a specific type of people; it wasn't designed for a specific race, profession, or only the intelligent. So, write your name among the greats. Stop being timid about success; embrace it, love it, and believe it. You are an icon, even if you never realised it. Walk like an icon; talk like an icon; act like an icon. BE AN ICON!

ABOUT THE AUTHOR

Kenneth Nkemnacho is a writer, teacher, mentor, inspirational speaker, and radio/television host. He has authored lots of books and articles which major on developing individuals for corporate excellence.

Kenneth is the CEO of Kenneth Vision Media; an organisation committed to writing, publishing, and content creations.

As a prolific blogger and social media expert, he founded www.successinks.com; a success and personal development blog that daily motivates and inspire people to beat the odds and excel in their chosen endeavours.

Kenneth is married to Ruth, and they are blessed with two children; Favour and Joshua.

If you would like him to feature as a speaker in your conferences, events, seminars, workshops, or training programmes, please send an email to Kenneth@kennethvisionmedia.com.